Jakarta Tourism, Indonesia

History, Environment, Security, Travel Guide and Information

Author
Caleb Gray.

SONITTEC PUBLISHING. All rights reserved. No part of this publication may be reproduced, distributed, or transmitted in any form or by any means, including photocopying, recording, or other electronic or mechanical methods, without the prior written permission of the publisher, except in the case of brief quotations embodied in critical reviews and certain other noncommercial uses permitted by copyright law. For permission requests, write to the publisher, addressed "Attention: Permissions Coordinator," at the address below.

Copyright © 2019 Sonittec Publishing
All Rights Reserved

First Printed: 2019.

ISBN:

Publisher:
SONITTEC LTD
College House, 2nd Floor
17 King Edwards Road,
Ruislip
London
HA4 7AE.

Table of Content

SUMMARY 1
INTRODUCTION 4
   LANDSCAPE 5
      City site 5
      Climate 5
      City layout 6
HISTORY 10
ECONOMY 14
   MANUFACTURING 14
   FINANCE AND OTHER SERVICES 14
   TRANSPORTATION 15
CULTURE 20
TRAVEL AND TOURISM 22
   INTERESTING PLACES 28
      Jakarta Old Town 32
      Pulau Seribu (Thousand Island) 35
         Air Kecil Island 37
         Alam Kotok Island 40
         Antuk Island 43
         Ayer Besar Island 45
         Biawak Island 48
         Bidadari Island 51
         Bintang Beach 54
         Bira Island 57
         Bokor Island 59
         Cangkir Island 62
         Cemara Kasih Kasih Beach 65
         Cipir Island 68
         Damar Besar Island 71
         Dolphin Island 74
         Genteng Island 76
         Gosong Rengat Island 79
         Harapan Island 82
         Hawksbill Sea Turtle Conservation 85
         Jukung Island 88
         Kelapa Island 91
         Kaliage Island 94
         Karang Island 96
         Karya Island 99
         Kelor Island 102
         King Pandita's Tombstone 105

- Kongsi Island 108
- Kresek Beach 111
- Laki Island 114
- Lancang Island 117
- Lipan Island 120
- Macan Island 123
- Matahari Island 126
- Melinjo Island 128

1945 Museum 131
Ancient Inscription Museum 133
Basoeki Abdullah Museum 134
Central Museum 137
Fantasy Land 138
Fine Art Museum 140
Indonesian Orchid Park 142
Indonesian Stamp Museum 145
Jakarta History Museum 148
Jakarta Museum of Kites 150
Jakarta Old Town 153
Jaya Ancol Dreamland 156
Keong Mas Park 158
Marina Jaya Ancol 161
Martha Tiahahu Park 162
Maritime Museum 165
National Monument 167
National Museum 168
Pancasila Sacred Monument 170
Ragunan Zoo 173
Sea World 176
Shadow Puppets Museum 177
Situ Babakan 180
Sunda Kelapa 183
T.I.M Art Center 185
TMII 186
Transportation Museum 187
Souvenir Center 191
Restaurants 193
Travel Agents 196

JAKARTA WEEKEND GUIDE 197

ACCOMMODATION 202
- Central Jakarta 203

- Kosenda Hotel 203
- Artotel 206
- Hotel Borobudur 209
- Konko Hostel 211
- Morrissey 214
- OYO 101 Apple Platinum Hotel 216
- Dreamtel 218

Kota Tua 221
- The Packer Lodge 221
- Wonderloft Hostel 224

Summary

The importance of travelling in our life?
Everyone has their very own reasons to travel. Some people travel for work, some travel for pleasure while for others it is just a way of life. They travel to live and to escape at the same time.

Whatever might be the reason to travel, here are few ways in which travelling would definitely change you and I think that is why travelling becomes so important in life:

<u>Enjoy being alone</u>: There is something therapeutic about being alone and being at peace with it. While you soak in a new culture, you also connect with your own inner self.

<u>Learn to adapt</u>: It is a different world out there, literally. Be it the pace of life, the language or simply the change in weather, it is always a change and you have to adapt to it. This is what makes travelling truly beautiful as you break away from the routine and adapt to something totally new.

Experience a new culture: Every place comes with its distinct cultural habits, you cannot think about New York without talking about its fast paced life and about Italy without enjoying its relaxed lifestyle. Similarly, while visiting the UK you might have to be a bit formal in your interactions with the locals, on the other hand, while greeting the people in Thailand, one can be really warm and casual.

Broaden your taste buds: Travelling without experiencing the local food is just not complete. It is not only a culinary experience but a cultural one as well.

Get out of comfort zone: From simple experiences like the weather, way of life or food to the more adventurous ones like trying a new sport, travelling really pushes ones boundaries to the core. You might end up participating in a street carnival in Brazil just like the locals or trying the local delicacies (read insects) in Thailand.

Indulge in Photography: It does not matter whether you are a professional or not. It is also irrelevant whether you have a DSLR or a very basic camera, while travelling what matters is the love and quest for seeing beautiful places and the sheer joy of capturing them in your lense. Travelling would in return give you your very own collection of amazing postcards of beautiful sunsets, snow laced mountains or sunny beaches.

<u>Learn to escape</u>: Travelling is the best way to break the routine. If you are in a bustling city, go ahead and experience the country life. If you are in a rural place, travel to a bustling city and experience its madness. Stressed with the city life or work pressure? A spa break in Himalayas or Kerala is a must try.

<u>Appreciate Nature</u>: The quest to explore more when one is travelling always leads to a sense of amazement about nature. While most of us keep a track of technological advancements, Nature has its own ways of outshining all of these. The Antelope Canyon in Arizona or Turquoise Ice in Russia are the finest examples of this. For more, check out the most unbelievable places around the world.

<u>Get closer to your own roots</u>: While one travels and experiences a lot of different cultures and practices, it definitely brings one closer to his or her own roots. Travel helps one appreciate one's identity and culture.

Travelling is all about experiences. They can happen in terms of culture, people, places but most importantly with one's own self and this was all about

Introduction

Jakarta, formerly (until 1949) Batavia or (1949–72) Djakarta, largest city and capital of Indonesia. Jakarta lies on the northwest coast of Java at the mouth of the Ciliwung (Liwung River), on Jakarta Bay (an embayment of the Java Sea). It is coextensive with the metropolitan district of Greater Jakarta (Jakarta Raya) and nearly coextensive with the *daerah khusus ibukota* (special capital district) of Jakarta the latter also including a number of small offshore islands in the Java Sea.

In 1966, when the city was declared a special capital district, it gained a status approximately equivalent to that of a state or province. The city has long been a major trade and financial centre. It has also become an important industrial city and a centre for education. Area special capital district, 255 square miles (661 square km). Pop. (2000) Greater Jakarta, 8,342,435;

special capital district, 8,361,079; (2010) Greater Jakarta, 9,586,705; special capital district, 9,607,787.

Landscape

City site

Jakarta lies on a low, flat alluvial plain with historically extensive swampy areas; the parts of the city farther inland are slightly higher. It is easily flooded during the rainy season. The draining of swamps for building purposes and the continuous decrease of upland forest vegetation have increased the danger of floods. With such an excess of water in the soil, Jakarta has a shortage of clean drinking water, for which there is increasing demand. The area is quite fertile for fruit and other horticulture, as most of the soil is of old volcanic origin.

Climate

Jakarta is a tropical, humid city, with annual temperatures ranging between the extremes of 75 and 93 °F (24 and 34 °C) and a relative humidity between 75 and 85 percent. The average mean temperatures are 79 °F (26 °C) in January and 82 °F (28 °C) in October. The annual rainfall is more than 67 inches (1,700 mm). Temperatures are often modified by sea winds. Jakarta, like any other large city, also has its share of air and noise pollution.

City layout

Although the Dutch were the first to attempt to plan the city, the city layout is probably more British than Dutch in character, as can be seen from such large squares as Medan Merdeka ("Freedom Field") and Lapangan Banteng (meaning "place of the gaur [large wild ox]"). The Oriental style, or "indische" style, as the Dutch call it, is apparent not only in the city's way of life but also in the types of houses, the wide, tree-lined streets, and the original spacious gardens and house lots. In Kebayoran, a satellite town built since World War II on the southwestern side of the city, and in other modern developments, the houses and garden lots are much smaller than in the older colonial districts.

Jakarta has long been a city of new settlers who assimilated local ways and became Jakartans themselves. Some traditional neighbourhoods can, however, be identified. The Kota ("City"; also called Kota Tua ["Old City"] or Old Batavia) area, sometimes called the downtown section, is the historical city centre, and it houses a significant part of the Chinese population. The contemporary city's business and financial hub lies somewhat to the south of Kota, primarily along Jenderal Sudirman and Mohammad Husni Thamrin roads, in central Jakarta. The area of Kemayoran ("Progress") and Senen, originally on the eastern fringe of the city, is now almost central in its location and increasingly has become the city's major retail area. The Jatinegara ("Real Country") section, originally a Sundanese settlement but later incorporated as a separate town, then a Dutch army camp (Meester Cornelis), is now merged with the rest of Jakarta and includes many new settlers. The Menteng and Gondangdia sections were formerly fashionable residential areas near the central Medan Merdeka (then called Weltevreden). To the west, Tanah Abang ("Red Earth") and Jati Petamburan are, like Kemayoran, densely developed. Tanjung Priok is the harbour, with its own community attached to it.

The most common type of house in the city is the kampong, or village, house; most such houses are built of materials such as wood or bamboo mats, but this does not necessarily mean that they are substandard. Another common type of housing, often used to house government workers, is the colonial urban house, or *rumah gedongan*; such houses are mostly single-family detached or semidetached, each standing on a separate lot. Apartment buildings constitute a more modern category;

although they are more economical in the use of land than single-family types, their architectural and construction costs often make them fairly expensive. Housing is generally overcrowded.

Some of Jakarta's buildings, such as the Portuguese Church (1695) in Kota, are of architectural or historical interest. Some of the buildings around the city square in Kota also date from colonial times, including the old city hall (1710), which has been restored and now serves as the municipal museum. The National Archives building was originally the palace of a Dutch governor-general, Abraham van Riebeeck. The Ministry of Finance building, facing Lapangan Banteng, also was designed as a governor's palace (Herman Willem Daendels, one of Napoleon's marshals). The Presidential Palace, north of Medan Merdeka, faces Monas, or Monumen Nasional (National Monument). The Istiqlal Mosque, in the northeast corner of Medan Merdeka opposite Lapangan Banteng, is one of the largest mosques in Southeast Asia. The National Museum (formerly the Central Museum), on the west side of Medan Merdeka, houses a collection of historical, cultural, and artistic artifacts.

After World War II Jakarta underwent a building boom. The Hotel Indonesia (the city's first high-rise building) and the Senayan Sports Complex were built for the Asian Gamesin 1962. Most high-rise buildings are located in the city's financial centre.

History

Jakarta's earliest history centres on the port of Sunda Kelapa, in the north of the modern city. When the Portuguese arrived in 1522, Sunda Kelapa was a bustling port of the Pajajaran dynasty, the last Hindu kingdom of West Java. By 1527 the Portuguese had gained a foothold in the city, but were driven out by Sunan Gunungjati, the Muslim saint and leader of Demak. He renamed the city Jayakarta, meaning 'victorious city', and it became a fiefdom of the Banten sultanate.

At the beginning of the 17th century the Dutch and English jostled for power in the city, and in late 1618 the Jayakartans, backed by the British, besieged the Vereenigde Oost-Indische Compagnie (VOC) fortress. The Dutch managed to fend off the attackers until May 1619 when, under the command of Jan Pieterszoon Coen, reinforcements stormed the town and reduced it to ashes. A stronger shoreline fortress was built and the town was renamed 'Batavia' after a tribe that once occupied parts of the Netherlands in Roman times. It soon became the capital of the Dutch East Indies.

Within the walls of Batavia the prosperous Dutch built tall houses and pestilential canals in an attempt to create an Amsterdam in the tropics. By the early 18th century, the city's population had swelled, boosted by both Indonesians and Chinese eager to take advantage of Batavia's commercial prospects.

By 1740 ethnic unrest in the Chinese quarters had grown to dangerous levels and on 9 October violence broke out on Batavia's streets; around 5000 Chinese were massacred. A year later Chinese inhabitants were moved to Glodok, outside the city walls. Other Batavians, discouraged by the severe epidemics between 1735 and 1780, also moved, and the city began to spread far south of the port.

Dutch colonial rule came to an end with the Japanese occupation in 1942 and the name 'Jakarta' was restored, but it wasn't until 1950 that Jakarta officially became the capital of the new republic.

Over the next four decades, the capital struggled under the weight of an ever-increasing population of poor migrants, but by the 1990s Jakarta's economic situation had turned around. This all changed, however, with the start of an economic collapse at the end of 1997. The capital quickly became a political battleground and protests demanding longtime leader Soeharto's resignation increased in intensity in early 1998.

After months of tension the floodgates opened on 12 May 1998 when the army fired live ammunition into a group of students at Trisakti University; four were killed. Jakarta erupted in three days of rioting as thousands took to the streets. The Chinese were hardest hit, with shocking tales of rape and murder emerging after the riots.

Over the past few years Jakarta has braved a spate of natural and unnatural disasters. In August 2003 the US-owned Marriott Hotel was bombed and in September 2004 Australia's embassy experienced a similar fate; both nations were targeted for their involvement in the Afghanistan and Iraq occupations. Flooding disabled many parts of the city in 2002, 2003 and 2006, causing massive damage to homes and public services, and bringing more misery to the abject poor.

However, the biggest problem facing the city may still be its ability to handle protesters. A proposed increase in fuel and utility prices in January 2003 caused thousands to hit the streets and forced the government to backtrack on its plans. However in October 2005 it went through with fuel increases amid widespread protests; fortunately military intervention was not required to maintain calm, but if fuel prices are raised once more violence could easily erupt on the streets of the capital.

Economy

Economically, Jakarta plays several roles. It can be identified first as the national capital and a central place of control for the national economy, then as an administrative centre in its own right, and as a significant industrial hub. In addition, its location as a port makes it an important centre for trade.

Manufacturing

Jakarta has some manufacturing industries. There are several iron foundries and repair shops, margarine and soap factories, and printing works. Machinery, cigarettes, paper, glassware, and wire cable as well as aluminum and asbestos and, more recently, automotive products are manufactured. There are also tanneries, sawmills, textile mills, food-processing plants, breweries, and a film industry.

Finance and other services

The cost of living in the city continues to rise. Land is expensive and rents are high. Industrial development and the construction of new housing are usually undertaken on the outskirts, while commerce and banking remain concentrated in the city centre. The Indonesian Chamber of Commerce is active in promoting trade with other countries; the annual Jakarta Fair (usually held from July to August) also serves to promote trade. Jakarta is the centre of roughly one-fourth of Indonesia's trade and services and two-thirds of its banking and financial sectors.

To meet the needs of the local city population, the municipality operates several markets. The central city markets (Pasar Kota), like the markets of Pasar Senen to the east of the central city and Pasar Glodok in the Kota area, are major retail centres. The Pasar Jatinegara is primarily a food supply centre. The district markets are fairly large, with each one catering to a whole section of the city. There are also small neighbourhood markets, each serving only a limited area. Special markets include one selling fish, one selling used and new automobile parts, the Pasar Rumput flea market, and the Jalan Surabayasouvenir and antique market. Jakarta also has several general neighbourhood markets.

Transportation

There are railways throughout Jakarta; however, they are inadequate in providing transportation for the citizens of Jakarta; during peak hours, the number of passengers simply exceeds its capacity. Railroads connect Jakarta to its neighboring cities: Depok and Bogor to the south, Tangerang and Serpong to the west, and Bekasi, Karawang, and Cikampek to the east. The major rail stations are Gambir, Jatinegara, Pasar Senen, Manggarai, Tanah Abang and Jakarta Kota.

Trans Jakarta operates a special bus-line called Busway. The Busway takes less than half an hour to traverse a route which would normally take more than an hour during peak hours. Construction of the 2nd and 3rd corridor routes of the Busway was completed in 2006, serving the route from Pulogadung to Kalideres. The busway serving the route from Blok M to Jakarta Kota has been operational since January 2004.

Despite the presence of many wide roads, Jakarta suffers from congestion due to heavy traffic, especially in the central business district. To reduce traffic jams, some major roads in Jakarta have a 'three in one' rule during rush hours, first introduced in 1992, prohibiting less than three passengers per car on certain roads. In 2005, this rule covered the Gatot Subroto Road. This ruling has presented an economic opportunity for "joki" (meaning "jockey"), who wait at the entry points to restricted areas and charge a fee to sit in cars which have only one or two occupants while they drive through.

Jakarta's roads are notorious for the undisciplined behavior of drivers; the rules of the road are broken with impunity and police bribery is commonplace. The painted lines on the road are regarded as mere suggestions, as vehicles often travel four or five abreast on a typical two-lane road, and it is not uncommon to encounter a vehicle traveling the wrong direction. In recent years, the number of motorcycles on the streets has been growing almost exponentially. The vast sea of small, 100-200cc motorcycles, many of which have 2-stroke motors, create much of the traffic, noise and air pollution that plague Jakarta.

An outer ring road is now being constructed and is partly operational from Cilincing-Cakung-Pasar Rebo-Pondok Pinang-Daan Mogot-Cengkareng. A toll road connects Jakarta to Soekarno-Hatta International Airport in the north of Jakarta. Also connected via toll road is the port of Merak and Tangerang to the west; and Bekasi, Cibitung and Karawang, Purwakarta and Bandung to the east.

Two lines of the Jakarta Monorail are planned: the green line serving Semanggi-Casablanca Road-Kuningan-Semanggi and the blue line serving Kampung Melayu-Casablanca Road-Tanah Abang-Roxy. In addition, there are plans for a two-line subway (MRT) system, with a north-south line between Kota and Lebak Bulus, with connections to both monorail lines; and an east-west line, which will connect with the north-south line at the Sawah Besar station. The current project, which began construction in 2005, has been halted due to a lack of funds and its future remains uncertain.

On June 6, 2007, the city administration introduced the Waterway, a new river boat service along the Ciliwung river, intended to reduce the traffic snarls in Jakarta. The two boats, each with a capacity of 28 passengers, travel 1.7 kilometres along the West Flood Canal between Halimun in South Jakarta and Karet in Central Jakarta

There are currently two airports serving Jakarta; Soekarno-Hatta International Airport (CGK) and Halim Perdanakusuma International Airport (HLP). Soekarno-Hatta International Airport is used for both private and commercial airliners connecting Jakarta with other Indonesian cities. It is also Indonesia's main international gateway. Halim Perdanakusuma International Airport serves mostly private and presidential flights.

Cycle rickshaws, called *becak* ("bechak"), provide local transportation in the back streets of some parts of the city. From the early 1940s to 1991 they were a common form of local transportation in the city. In 1966, an estimated 160,000 rickshaws were operating in the city; as much as fifteen percent of Jakarta's total workforce was engaged in rickshaw driving. In 1971, rickshaws were banned from major roads, and shortly thereafter the government attempted a total ban, which substantially reduced their numbers but did not eliminate them. An especially aggressive campaign to eliminate them finally succeeded in 1990 and 1991, but during the economic crisis of 1998, some returned amid less effective government attempts to control them. The only place left in Jakarta where riding becak is permitted is the amusement park *Taman Impian Jaya Ancol.*

Culture

As the economic and political capital of Indonesia, Jakarta attracts many foreign as well as domestic immigrants. As a result, Jakarta has a decidedly cosmopolitan flavor and a diverse culture. Many of the immigrants are from the other parts of Java, bringing along a mixture of dialects of the Javanese and Sundanese languages, as well as their traditional foods and customs. The Betawi (Orang Betawi, or "people of Batavia") is a term used to describe the descendants of the people living around Batavia since around the eighteenth century. The Betawi people are mostly descended from various Southeast Asian ethnic groups brought or attracted to Batavia to meet the demand for labor, and includes people from various parts of Indonesia. The language and culture of these immigrants are distinct from those of the Sundanese or Javanese. There has also been a Chinese community in Jakarta for centuries. Officially they make up 6 percent of the Jakarta population, though this number may be under- reported.[17]

Jakarta has several performing arts centers, including the Senayan center. Traditional music, including wayang and gamelanperformances, can often be heard at high-class hotels. As the largest Indonesian city, Jakarta has lured talented musicians and artisans from many regions, who come to the city hoping to find a greater audience and more opportunities for success.

The concentration of wealth and political influence in the city means that foreign influence on its landscape and culture, such as the presence of international fast-food chains, is much more noticeable than in the more rural areas of Indonesia.

Travel and Tourism

Pollution choked, traffic clogged, drowning in its own swampy mire, it may seem it has very little to love, but, despite what decades of guidebooks have been telling people, relax, not everyone is out to scam you Jakarta is often a genuinely friendly city, in fact it's known as a "big kampung" and is indeed perhaps the world's biggest "village". The city's open-hearted citizens will talk to you on public transport, yell hello in the street and even cross the road just to shake your hand where else does that happen in a modern city? And one with around ten million inhabitants to boot!

It is true that Jakarta has massive infrastructure challenges, and the traffic jams can be absolutely appalling, but an MRT project is well on the way, and other public transport systems have been slowly improved over the last decade. Despite the challenges and dysfunction the predominant undercurrent of this megatropolis is optimism most people just get on with the business of living, often with a smile on their face however challenging life can be for some here and the city seems to function as if it were a living entity.

The city is not only a microcosm of Indonesia, the embodiment of the national motto "Unity in Diversity", but also a microcosm of emotion, sure it can be bewildering at times but in equal measures Jakarta has plenty to delight and beguile even the most sceptical of travellers, you may even want to stay an extra day.

Jakarta is officially called "Daerah Khusus Ibu Kota Jakarta" abbreviated as DKI (the Special Capital Region of Jakarta), located on the northwest coast of Java and is the nation's centre of economics, politics and power. The city was likely established as the trading port by the Hindu Sundanese Kingdom, perhaps as early as the first century, known as Sunda Kelapa. From here spices were shipped to the rest of the world, with local pepper being particularly prized and even today the port remains active in the city's north.

Over the centuries the constant battle for dominance of the lucrative spice trade saw power shift to Java's Islamic kingdoms who renamed the port "Jayakarta" meaning "The glorious victory" (or some such hyperbole), the Portuguese, the English and eventually at the beginning of the 17th century, the Dutch took control and renamed the port Batavia, planned and built a walled city and for the next 300 years ran their mighty mercantile empire from the area know today as "Kota Tua". By the mid-18th century constant bouts of malaria from the swampy canals saw the city grow as people moved to healthier areas to the south.

World War II brought the Japanese invasion, and finally at the end of occupation in 1942 the name Jakarta (a contraction of "Jayakarta") was installed. Indonesia gained independence in 1945 and Jakarta became the capital of the new nation. The southern area established by the Dutch was designated the official city centre and a post-independence fervour to glorify the republic saw mass construction of modern monuments and public buildings. The city continued to grow rapidly and mostly unplanned until the sprawling urban mess became indistinguishable from its satellite cities. Today the greater urban area is known as Jabodetabekfor Jakarta, Bogor, Depok, Tangerang and Bekasi and has a combined population of more than 30 million inhabitants.

Alongside Jakarta's modern buildings and shopping malls, much of the early Dutch architecture survives and Kota Tua, the old walled city of Batavia, has been redeveloped and many buildings have undergone restoration and reopened as museums. For most visitors arriving in Jakarta, this is an interesting area to explore along with the nearby port of Sunda Kelapa where you can still see old wooden pinisi ships.

Heading south, Glodok is Jakarta's Chinatown established in 1740 when the Dutch forced the Chinese out from the walled city. Here you'll find temples and some excellent street food. Around the modern city centre, take the opportunity to see one of Southeast Asia's finest collections of antiquities and curiosities at the National Museum, take a bird's-eye view of the city from Monas, the National Monument or just wander around the city square and soak up the atmosphere. Visit the modern Istiqlal Mosque the largest in Southeast Asia and discover a number of historic churches too.

For lovers of the arts, learn about Indonesian modern Art at Galeri Nasional Indonesia and the Museum Tekstil Jakarta may be of interest to some or join the queues at one of the private contemporary art museums, Museum MACAN or Art:1. Antique aficionados may want to have a potter around Jalan Surabaya Flea Market a little south of the city centre.

To get your bearings, join a pay-as-you-wish walking tour with Jakarta Good Guides or simply pick up some maps and brochures at the Visitors Information Centre (but do double check what they tell you). Once you have done seeing the official "sights", discover Jakarta's true heart step back from the glitzy malls and glass-fronted skyscrapers and head to the backstreets and kampungs, pull up a stool in one of the ubiquitous warungs or street stalls, order a steaming bowl of *Soto Betawi* or a strong *Kopi Jawa* and in no time one of Jakarta's famously congenial residents will start up a conversation, you may even make a lifelong friend.

Jakarta offers a smorgasbord of culinary choice from across the nation and across the world from Michelin Star restaurants to street food and everything in between, and the bar and nightclub scene thrives despite certain political factions chagrin. If you're in town on an expense account, you'll have no trouble finding excellent accommodation, but for budget travellers the pickings are somewhat less bountiful, but there is still comfort to be found.

Jakarta's public transport system may seem daunting at first, but commuter trains and the TransJakarta Busway are surprisingly efficient and friendly folk will point you in the right direction (you'll avoid the "macet" too), or there is always Go-Jek or a taxi. This notorious "macet" (traffic jam) is somewhat alleviated on weekends, when Jakarta becomes generally calmer and less frantic. The city centre enjoys a car free day every Sunday from 06:00 to 11:00 and it's fun to join in the action as thousands walk, run, cycle and skate on the street. Many hotels offer discounted rates on weekends and if you can, this is the best time to plan your visit to the capital.

If your intent is to travel to Bandung or Bogor on the weekend, we would seriously consider changing your itinerary or adding another night in Jakarta (really, there's plenty to see), as that midweek traffic has simply moved to these satellite cities along with half of the population of Jakarta.

When you do want to get out of town, Gambir, the main intercity train station at the southeastern corner of Merdeka Square has frequent connections to Bandung, Yogyakarta, Semarang and Surabaya. It's from here that you can also catch a bus to the airport. Trains to Bogor are on the commuter route from any commuter station. The main bus terminals are all far outside the city centre, but connected to the TransJakarta busway although trains are generally the better bet when moving on from Jakarta.

Interesting Places
Places of interest

Jakarta is the capital city of the Republic of Indonesia, a country composed of more than 13,000 islands with a population of over 180 million. Comprising more than 300 ethnic groups speaking 200 different languages, the Indonesia population exhibits marked diversity in its linguistic, culture, and religious traditions. As the Capital City, Jakarta is a melting pot of representatives from each of these ethnic groups. Jakarta is a special territory enjoying the status of a province, consisting of Greater Jakarta, covering of 637.44 square km area. Located on the northern coast of West Java, it is the center of government, commerce and industry and has an extensive communications network with the rest of the country and the outside world. Strategically positioned in the archipelago, the city is also the principal gateway to the rest of Indonesia. From the Capital City, sophisticated land, air, and sea transport is available to the rest of the country and beyond.

Jakarta is one of Indonesia's designated tourist areas. It is a gateway to other tourist destinations in Indonesia and is equipped with all the means of modern transportation by air, sea, rail, or by land. It has the largest and most modern airport in the country, the most important harbor in Indonesia and is well connected by rail of good roads to other destinations in Java, Sumatra, and Bali. As Indonesia's main gateway, Soekarno-Hatta International Airport serves a growing number of international airlines and domestic flights. Jakarta is a city of contrasts; the traditional and the modern, the rich and the poor, the sacral and the worldly, often stand side by side in this bustling metropolis. Even its population gathered from all those diverse ethnic and cultural groups, which compose Indonesia, are constantly juxtaposed present reminder of the national motto; Unity in Diversity.

Finding its origin in the small early 16th century harbor town of Sunda Kelapa, Jakarta's founding is thought to have taken place on June 22, 1527, when it was re-named Jayakarta, meaning Glorious Victory by the conquering Prince Fatahillah from neighboring Cirebon. The Dutch East Indies Company, which captured the town and destroyed it in 1619, changed its name into Batavia and made it the center for the expansion of their power in the East Indies. Shortly after the outbreak of World War II, Batavia fell into the hands of the invading Japanese forces that changed the name of the city into 'Jakarta' as a gesture aimed at winning the sympathy of the Indonesians. The name was retained after Indonesia achieved national independence after the war's end.

The ethnic of Jakarta called "Orang Betawi" speaks Betawi Malay, spoken as well in the surrounding towns such as Bekasi and Tangerang. Their language, Betawi Malay, has two variations: conventional Betawi Malay, spoken by elder people and bred in Jakarta, and modern Jakarta Malay, a slang form spoken by the younger generation and migrants.

Bunderan HI

Jakarta's architecture reflects to a large extent the influx of outside influences, which came and has remained in this vital seaport city. Taman Fatahillah Restoration Project, begun in the early 1970s has restored one of the oldest sections of Jakarta also known as Old Batavia to approximately its original state. The Old Portuguese Church and warehouse have been rehabilitated into living museums. The old Supreme Court building is now a museum of fine arts, which also houses part of the excellent

Chinese porcelain collection of former Vice President Adam Malik. The old Town Hall has become the Jakarta Museum, displaying such rare items as Indonesia's old historical documents and Dutch period furniture. Its tower clock was once returned to England to be repaired under its lifetime guarantee, which up to now has already lasted hundreds of years.

In recent years, Jakarta has expanded its facilities for visitors with luxury hotels, fine restaurants, exciting nightlife and modern shopping centers. It contains many tourist attractions such as Taman Mini Indonesia Indah (Beautiful "Indonesia in Miniature" Park), restored colonial period buildings, island resorts in the Pula Seribu (Thousand Island), and an extensive beach recreation complex called Ancol. "Beautiful Indonesia in Miniature Park" popularly called TMII "Taman Mini Indonesia Indah", built to portray the variety of cultures found within the many islands contained in the Republic of Indonesia, this open-air museum comprises the many architectural forms of arts and traditions of all Indonesia provinces. It is proof of the country's motto of Unity in Diversity as well as Freedom of Religion depicted in the houses of worship built on the grounds.

Jakarta has preserved its past and is developing for the future. Skyscrapers in the center of the city are part of a new look. Modern luxury hotels today cater to the discriminating visitors. Transport within the city is plentiful. Jakarta is the center of the nation's industrial, political and cultural life. It is home to many of the country's finest research institutes, educational facilities, and cultural organizations. Jakarta is uniquely the seat of both the national as well as the regional government.

Over the last several decades, Jakarta has proudly developed into one of Asia's most prominent metropolitan centers. Today, Jakarta's skyline is covered by modern high rises. The many state-of-the-art shopping centers, recreation complexes and toll-roads have become hallmarks of the city. The quality of life and the general welfare of its inhabitants have improved considerably with the city's fast pace of development. Jakarta's cultural richness and dynamic growth contribute significantly to its growing importance as one of the world's leading capital cities.

Jakarta Old Town

Jakarta is the capital of a beautiful country called Indonesia and it has become a center of government for decades. Aside from being a business and governance center, it also has a splendid history and culture. For example, there is one called Kota Tua or Old Old Town. As the name suggests, it holds numerous historic structures, which were used during the colonialism era. The fact is Jakarta (Batavia) was once considered a strategic spot to trade during the 16th century. Today, the site becomes tourists' favorite destination to hang out and feel the old atmosphere of the city.

The Nuance

Kota Tua Jakarta or the Old Town of Jakarta is located in Kunir Street 23 A, Tamansari. It belongs to West Jakarta City, actually. Despite the small size, which is about 1.3 km2, it has lots of attractions including historical buildings and several spots to hang out. Most of the structures are old museums, but an old harbor also resides near to the area. Tourists usually come there during the afternoon or at night when the nuance feels more comfortable. Some people are also seen in the morning as they enjoy fresh air and do some sports like jogging.

Exploring Jakarta Old Town

Due to its historic atmosphere, Jakarta Old Town is suitable for walking around and jogging. That means visitors can take advantage of the nuance to find peace and eradicate stresses. They can explore the area and see numerous old buildings land museums. Some parts of it are used by local vendors to promote their items, as well. These include foods, accessories, etc. For those who want to visit the museums, they must come before 3 pm (the closing hour). The thing is they should avoid coming at noon when the temperature is hot. Thus, the best time to visit is in the morning.

The main charm of Old Town is the formation of old museums, which are scattered near to each other. These include Bank Mandiri, Bank Indonesia, Arts & Ceramics, and Wayang Museum. Each of them offers distinct beauty so tourists should visit them all. As mentioned before, visitors should come before the closing hour. For those who look for a simpler activity, they can enjoy riding a bike around the area. Have no worries. Some locals provide bikes for rent to tourists and the price is quite affordable.

Another unique attraction in Jakarta Old Town is the presence of local artists, those who dress like a statue, soldiers, Dutch lady, and much more. They move around the area and often become an object for photography. Visitors are even allowed to take pictures with them, in fact. At the end of the adventure, tourists should enjoy local snacks called Kerak Telor. It is both crispy and tasty!

Nearby Attractions

- ✓ ITC Mangga Dua
- ✓ Mangga Dua Morning Market

How to Get There

The best transportation service to use to reach Kota Tua Jakarta (Jakarta Old Town) is the commuter line. The fact is that the area is accessible from any location, so it is quite reachable. For those who don't want to feel any hassle, riding a taxi is the simplest way to head to the site despite the expensive fee.

Where to Stay

- ✓ Ibis Mangga Dua Hotel
- ✓ RedDoorz Hotel

Pulau Seribu (Thousand Island)

Thousand Isles near Jakarta has been a favorite destination for ages. Paradiso, containing four island's Kahyangan (formerly known as Cipir), Bidadari (used to be called Sakit), Onrust and

Kelor offer spectacular views of the forest and the sea. The name Paradiso indeed comes from Paradise, for 'Kahyangan' in Indonesian means 'Heaven' in English, and 'Bidadari' means 'Angel'. Dotted throughout Jakarta Bay are 120 tropical islands and coral atolls known, rather misleadingly, as the Thousand Islands. This group of islands in the Jakarta Bay offers a heaven away from the bustle of city life. There are golden beaches fringed with coconut palms. The surrounding waters are a paradise for skin divers. They are filled with a myriad of tropical fish, which live among the multicolored corals. The islands can be reached from Tanjung Priok or Pasar Ikan (Sunda Kelapa) by ferry or by chartered boat. Some of the islands in this group developed for tourism are Pulau Bidadari, Pulau Anyer, Pulau Laki and Pulau Putri. Pulau Tanjung near Putri has an airstrip. There are cabins for hire, having fresh water on Pulau Air and Pulau Bidadari only. The Pulau Putri Paradise Co. has developed Pulau Putri, Pulau Melintang, Pulau Petondan and Pulau Papa Theo as a holiday resort with cottages, restaurants, diving and sailing facilities. With a total population of only 13,000 people, the bay contains a sprinkling of the 'virgin islands', although the majorities are inhabited. Many are privately owned. The departure point to this cluster of individual paradises is the Ancol

Marina, where further information on travel arrangements can be found. Daliy boats to most islands, departing at 08.00 and 09.00.

This chain of several dozen islets immediately north of the city is administratively part of Jakarta and usually an oasis of quiet. Speedboats take visitors to basic but comfortable hotels an hour or so from the city, where one can snorkel, dive or just lie on a white sand beach with a friendly turtle.

Air Kecil Island

A Vanished Air Kecil Island in Thousand Islands Regency
Air Kecil or Ayer Island was part of Thousand Islands Regency. It was located near to Air Besar Island and Jakarta. Today, tourists come to the location to explore its reminiscences. Also, travelers would love to learn its history. If you are visiting "Kepulauan Seribu", you must never miss such opportunity. According to locals, Air Kecil is also called Jusi Island. Due to illegal sand mining, the island vanished. The sibling, Air Besar Island, is also popular actually. It becomes an alternative to enjoy a great vacation in Indonesia.

The Nuance

When it comes to physical appearance, Ayer Kecil Island was a beautiful isle. It consists of white sand and several types of floras. However, you won't find it anymore. The island was totally ruined. What you can see is only the location or spot where the island was present. The waves erased the existence of the island. Despite this fact, many tourists keep coming to such location. Perhaps they don't believe such fact. Some of them only want to explore beautiful spots near to the location. Snorkeling is popular there.

Exploring Air Kecil Island

Just because there is no land, doesn't mean Air Kecil is a bad place for a vacation. On the other hand, it attracts many visitors over time. Why is that? You can take advantage of its nautical beauty. From Air Besar Island, you can take your snorkeling gear and head to Air Kecil territory. The seawater is good for snorkeling there. Not to mention you can rent the local boat easily. The underwater views are the main attraction in such tourist spot!

Next adventure is the boat trip. It is a special voyage, so you can enjoy the journey. Reaching both Ayer Kecil and Besar Island is worth a try. The environment is definitely refreshing. One thing, you should use a comfortable boat. For the best experience, there is a speedboat. It is considered a better option. The thing is you must pay more for it. The price is cheaper if you come with more people. That means all of you can chip in.

Once you explore the reminiscences of Air Kecil Island, it is time to visit the brother. The name is Air Besar Island. It is famous for its cottages. There are both land and floating cottages. All of them are comfortable. All visitors are going to have good times there. So, what's next? You should try traditional culinary. Thousand Islands Regency is the home of delicious foods. Toothless gum chips are included. Fish chips are also recommended. They taste great!

Nearby Attractions

- Jakarta
- Tanjung Pasir Beach
- Edam Island

How to Get There

In order to reach Ayer Kecil and Besar Island, you must use a boat from Muara Angke. In the port, there are many choices of boats to ride. You can either choose traditional or speedboats. Each of them costs differently, as well. Apart from Muara Angke, you can depart from Marina Ancol Port. For your information, it is the home of speedboats. Make sure you carry much money!

Where to Stay

> Ayer Resort and Cottages

Alam Kotok Island

An Amusing Nature in Alam Kotok Island, Thousand Islands Regency

Jakarta holds a beautiful archipelago in the Java Sea. The name is Thousand Islands Regency. As the name implies, it is the home of tons of isles. One of them is called Alam Kotok. Despite its unique name, no one knows the meaning. Another name is Kulkul Kotok. The island is famous for its nature tourism. It features lots of natural attractions and beautiful landscapes. People also visit it due to a great visibility of the sea. No wonder, the island becomes a lure for divers.

The Nuance

A peaceful impression of Kotok Island is common. It has several unique characteristics such as traditional and sultry. Once you have arrived at the island, the locals may offer you a fresh coconut drink. It is quite refreshing! In the seashore, there are mangroves and several types of trees. Not to mention there are some exotic animals, too. These include lizards, birds, and much more. When it comes to the beach, the sand is soft and comfortable. It creates an amazing and romantic nuance. If you love diving, you can enjoy nautical beauty likes colorful corals.

Exploring Alam Kotok Island

Kulkul Kotok Resort radiates an unspoiled beauty. Due to this reason, it is suitable for those who look for a solemn vacation destination. That means you can retreat from your daily routines. No wonder, many people in Jakarta often visit the island. The best spot to explore is the beach. You can find bungalows near to the shorelines, as well. Those become a great spot for relaxation. It feels like you are living in a tree house! With a few minutes of sightseeing, you can overcome your stresses.

In the afternoon, it is time for beach walking. The sand is safe for your feet. You can even walk barefoot on it. Do you love nautical beauty? In this case, diving and snorkeling are recommended. From the pier, you can ride a boat to several diving spots. Make sure to wear proper gears! Once you explore the sea, you should go back to the island. As an alternative, you are able to continue your adventure to Kotok Kecil Island. It is situated near to the big one, after all.

Along the way, you may see several dolphins. They are a perfect companion to reach your destination. Once you reach such small island, there is only a deserted land and plants. No worries. It is suitable for self-reflection. Before evening, you must head back to Kotok Besar. It is time to rest in the resort. Don't forget to enjoy delicious foods, especially Gepuk Skewer.

Nearby Attractions

- Simpul Island
- Kelapa Island
- Opak Island

How to Get There

Alam Kotok Island is located near to Simpul Island. Mostly, travelers depart from Muara Angke. However, many tourists are looking for a faster trip. In this case, you can use Marina Ancol Port. From here, you can rent a speedboat. The trip takes about 90 minutes. It depends on the weather, as well. According to the schedule, the speedboat departs at 8 am in the morning. Make sure you come early!

Where to Stay

- Alam Kotok Resort

Antuk Island

Antuk Island in Thousand Islands Regency, Jakarta
As an archipelago country, Indonesia becomes the home of many islands. In the Java Sea, you can find Thousand Islands Regency. It is part of Jakarta Special Region, actually. As the name implies, it holds lots of isles. One of them is called Antuk. Another name is Pantara. It is located near to Sepa Island. It consists of East and West Pantara. Tourists come to the island to enjoy a wonderful ambiance of nature. If you want to visit a Japanese restaurant, you should go to the west one. Unfortunately, it is no longer operated. Today, only East Antuk is often visited by tourists.

The Nuance

In East Pantara or Antuk Island, you can enjoy flawless nature. The sky is pure and it is reflected on the water. There is a wooden pier. Tourists often use to sightsee nearby scenery. Near to it, you can find several speedboats. They are ready to help you reach neighboring islands. In the sea, there are several big rocks, as well. They become a unique addition to the beach. In some occasions, you may see several people fishing. If necessary, you can join them.

Exploring Antuk Island

The first thing to do in Antuk Island is watersports. Due to beautiful beaches, it becomes an ideal location for jet skiing, riding the banana boat, snorkeling, fishing, canoeing, etc. Moreover, you don't even need to carry your own gears. It is because you can rent them in the resort. For those who want to ride a jet ski, it is better to carry much money. In holidays, the price becomes more expensive. No wonder, it is because there are more visitors at that time.

Next, it is the children playground. For those who come with kids, Antuk Island provides a special location for kids. Kiddos can play numerous games there. The playground is surrounded by trees, as well. That means the children can play in it comfortably. Once you have explored all parts of the island, it is time to rest in the cottage. There are numerous facilities provided such as a swimming pool, a bar, a restaurant, etc.

In the morning, you can witness a beautiful sunrise in the shorelines. As an alternative, you can see it from the resort. Don't forget to eat your breakfast there. You can taste delicious and traditional menus. At the last day of your vacation, you should drop by in West Antuk. There is the reminiscence of a Japanese restaurant. The island was popular back then. Though, it is no longer available. What you can find is only an isolated atmosphere. Though, it is a good place for finding peace and self-reflecting.

Nearby Attractions

- Sepa Island

How to Get There

It is going to be a long trip. From Tanjung Kait, you can take a traditional motor boat. Along the way, you may pass several islands. Antuk or Pantara Island is situated in the northernmost of "Kepulauan Seribu". For a faster trip, you can depart from Marina Ancol. It takes about 2 hours to reach the island using a speedboat.

Where to Stay

- East Antuk Resort

Ayer Besar Island

Enjoying a Great Resort in Ayer Besar Island, Jakarta
Ayer Besar Island makes a wonderful vacation spot for everyone. The location is in Thousand Island Regency, Jakarta. The best feature is the resort. It is popular both for domestic and foreign tourists, as well. In Ayer Besar, you can find several cottages. Those apply a traditional architecture. The roof is made of sago

palm leaves. The best thing is tourists are allowed to rent a whole cottage for themselves. Apart from land cottages, you can also find water cottages. As the name suggests, these are built on a watery terrain.

The Nuance

As mentioned earlier, Ayer Besar Island is famous for its resort. Near to it, there is a solid pier. It represents a well-maintained facility. The resort is surrounded by trees and small gardens. When it comes to seawater, it has a green color. There are no big waves, so it is safe for swimming. Still, most of the visitors come here for leisure. The resort offers the best facilities and comfortable amenities. In a nutshell, it is a paradise for travelers.

Exploring Ayer Besar Island

For those who love challenging activities, Ayer Besar Island can be a wonderful destination since it features a wild terrain. For some reasons, many backpackers often come there. You can come with friends or families. Nature tourism is a primary attraction in Ayer Besar. Make sure you don't miss such opportunity. In the docks, there are several boats. You can hop in and explore nearby islands, too. Not to mention there are numerous facilities such as a restaurant, cottage, karaoke bar, and souvenir vendors.

Next, there is a unique characteristic of Ayer Besar Island. It is Ojar Stage. The locals call it Panggung Ojar. Actually, it is a replica of a sailing boat. Also, it becomes the center of attraction. If you come at the right time, you can witness several events. Apart from that, the island features entertainment systems. If you want to relax, you can find several cottages in Ayer Besar. These include floating and land cottages. Both of them offer high-quality facilities, though.

Not all facilities in Ayer Besar Island are pricey. Though, you shouldn't be stingy. For the best services and amenities, you should spend more money on them. What about backpackers? Well, you shouldn't have to spend money. Getting fun in Ayer Besar can be done freely, after all. For instance, you can sit on the beach and witness the nature. The sound of waves is definitely mesmerizing. This is a free activity so it costs nothing.

Nearby Attractions

- Ayer Kecil Island
- Bira Island

How to Get There

In order to reach Ayer Besar Island, you must head to Muara Angke. This is your first destination. From the port, you can pick any boat. Even though it takes longer than a speedboat, it is worth a ride. Also, you can enjoy the journey in a comfortable manner. Not to mention the price is cheaper than a speedboat. Once you reach Ayer Island, you can explore it freely. If you want more adventures, you can visit nearby islands, actually.

Where to Stay

- Ayer Resort

Biawak Island

Biawak Island in Thousand Islands Regency, Jakarta

Not all tourists have heard about Biawak Island. It is one of the recommended isles in Thousand Islands Regency. Biawak means "lizard". No wonder, you may encounter many lizards in some parts of the island. Actually, there is another name. It is Rakit Island. Many people called it that way in the past. When it comes to the location, the island is situated about 40 km from Java Island, especially Indramayu. The government has chosen it as natural conservation for wild lizards. Today, it becomes one of the best lures in "Kepulauan Seribu".

The Nuance

The sea has moderate waves. Still, it is possible to swim in it. Several traditional boats are often seen nearby. These accommodate visitors either from Java or other places. In terms of appearance, the island is covered mostly by trees. Due to this reason, it is a little bit difficult to explore all parts of the isle. There are only several paths, though. For beginners, it is better to come with a tour guide. This person helps you explore the island in an efficient manner.

Exploring Biawak Island

Once you reach the island, the first thing to do is to climb ZM Willem III lighthouse. It is an icon of Biawak Isle, after all. Despite its old age, the tower remains functional. It was built in 1872, actually. The lighthouse's height is 65 meters and there are 17 levels on it. In terms of appearance, it looks old but gorgeous. The stairs are narrow, so you must be careful when climbing them. In the top, the scenery is jaw-dropping. Make sure to carry a camera, so you can capture great objects from above.

Next adventure is in the forest. There is natural conservation for lizards. The local name of such creature is Biawak, actually. For the best experience, it is better to hire a tour guide beforehand.

This way, you can get information regarding that place. Not to mention you can get around the location efficiently. It will be different if you go alone. As for the tip, there are lots of mosquitos living there. Make sure to wear proper clothes and apply a repellent.

Another thing to do is on the pier. You can do many things there. It is as simple as enjoying sea scenery. In some occasions, you should try fishing. As long as you carry a fishing rod and baits, you are ready to go. If you come at the right time, you can enjoy either a beautiful sunset or sunrise. If you love snorkeling, there are some good spots nearby. Once again, you must have prepared the gears beforehand.

Nearby Attractions

- Indramayu

How to Get There

From Jakarta, you need to head to Indramayu. Your destination is Muara Karangasong. From there, you can directly head to Biawak Island. The trip takes about 5 hours. The waves are strong, so it is going to be a rough trip. Have no fear. It is worth an effort. At the end, it rewards you with a great island called Biawak! Have a nice trip.

Where to Stay

➢ Hotels in Indramayu

Bidadari Island

A Historical Spot in Jakarta - The Angel Island aka Bidadari Island

In a Thousand Islands Regency, you can find a unique place called Angel Island. Though, the locals call it Bidadari Island. In the past, it's called Sakit Island. What is good in there? You can find a recognizable icon, which is the cottage. The island has both land and water cottages, after all. The island features beautiful scenery and solemn nuance. Not to mention it is the closest island to Jakarta. That means tourists can reach it without hassles. Most of the visitors are attracted to the Martello Fort.

The Nuance

Angel Island features an old fort. It becomes an icon of the island, in fact. There are not many trees or plants there. It is because the island has a small size. The location is also near to Jakarta Port. Thus, you can look for hotels easily. Apart from a historic fort, Bidadari Island has stunning beach views. In the seashore, you can sit and witness some boats. Those vessels go back and forth attractively. You can also simply enjoy the nuance in the shorelines. The breezy wind makes you relaxed, for sure.

Exploring Bidadari Island

Martello Fort attracts more visitors over time. It was an important structure in the 17th century, after all. Today, it becomes the main feature in Bidadari Island. Due to its popularity, the fort suits a photography background. You may expect several photographers there. Apart from taking photos, you can do other things like diving, swimming, and snorkeling. Thanks to beautiful and calm seawater. Another popular activity is island hopping. People also call it 3 Cruise Island. The nearby islands are Kelor, Khayangan, and Onrust.

Next, there is a unique landmark in Angel Island. It is "Tanduk Tujuh Belas" Statue. It is actually a deer statue. The upper half of the body is deer and the lower part is fish. What a unique figure! As the name suggests, such statue has 17 horns. The color is white and it has a unique pose. The deer figure lifts its front legs. Tourists often make it as a photography background or object. Next, there are several rare plants. It is an opportunity to witness those unique floras directly.

Once you have explored different parts of the island, it is time to eat! There is a traditional restaurant in Angel Island. The most famous culinary is Gepuk Skewer. It is made of mackerel tuna. When it comes to flavor, it tastes spicy and savory. The other local foods are stir-fry squids, fish pastel, talam fish cake, and much more. Make sure you try them all!

Nearby Attractions

- Kelor Island
- Khayangan Island
- Onrust Island

How to Get There

There are many types of boats available. You can ride one to reach Bidadari Island. The most common one is a wooden boat. Some tourists choose Kerapu boats, though. Also, there are several speedboats. These are considered the fastest. First, you must head to Muara Angke Port. As alternatives, there are Marina Ancol and Muara Kamal Port. The best time to depart is in the morning. The atmosphere is cool and you can even see a sunrise.

Where to Stay

- Bidadari Resort
- Nef Tour

Bintang Beach

Visiting Bintang Beach in Pari Island, Thousand Islands Regency

Pari Island is part of "Kepulauan Seribu". In terms of beauty, the island is indeed satisfying. Most people visit it for relaxation and enjoying the nautical beauty. One of the best attractions in Pari is Bintang Beach. Bintang means "star". It is because you can find many starfishes on the coast. They come in different size and color, actually. Another name of the location is Star Beach. The location is about 400 meters from Pari's Dock. It is suitable for beach walking and relaxation!

The Nuance

Once you reach the island, you can feel clean and soothing ambiance. The beauty of Star Beach gives you a comfortable mood, for sure. Thanks to the management team. There is no trash at all. Near to the beach, you can find several pine trees. They create a soothing atmosphere. With these features, you can relax wholeheartedly. On top of that, there are several traditional halls and hammocks nearby. You can use them for relaxation. No wonder, you can spend hours in Bintang Beach.

Exploring Bintang Beach

A vacation in Pari Island is incomplete without visiting Star Beach. It's common sense. You can simply sit in the small park with stunning sea scenery. Though, the best attraction is definitely the starfishes. They become the main feature of the beach, after all. Not to mention they become a primary attraction there. Tourists are allowed to take pictures with their camera. If you are brave enough, you can touch those creatures! Some of them are safe to touch, indeed.

Beach walking is a good idea. Thanks to Bintang Beach's cleanliness and soothing nuance. Tourists can enjoy a flawless atmosphere in Star Beach. Not to mention it features soft and beautiful sand. You can go barefoot with no worries. If you want to avoid the heat, there are some canopies. During a holiday, more people come there. Make sure not to miss the canopy! For the best comfort, you can relax on the hammock. You can find some under the trees.

The thing is you can't swim in the water. The shorelines are too shallow. That means it doesn't accommodate swimmers. On the other hand, you can simply play water and reach several starfishes. In the afternoon, you must never miss the sunset. Usually, tourists enjoy a cup of coffee while enjoying such stunning sunset. Here is the thing. The beach doesn't feature good lighting. Thus, you should get back before evening. Also, you must come at the right time. Summer is the best time to visit Pari Island and Star Beach. If you expect many people, you must come during holidays or weekends.

Nearby Attractions

- Lancang Island
- Kongsi Island

How to Get There

There are two methods to reach Bintang Beach. First, it is from Muara Angke. A traditional motorboat will take you to Pari Island. Once you get there, you must walk about 400 meters to reach the beach. Another method is from Marina Ancol, it is a faster route to reach Pari. Though, a speedboat costs more than regular boats. Make sure to prepare enough money. Enjoy your trip!

Where to Stay

- Cottages in Untung Jawa Island

Bira Island

An Untouched Beauty in Bira Island, Jakarta

If you are visiting A Thousand Archipelago, you must never miss Bira Island. It is one of the best isles in such regency, after all. Bira becomes tourists' favorite location for beach walking and an underwater adventure. Despite its popularity, you don't see many visitors in that island. This way, you can take advantage of it for relaxation. The nuance is solemn and it features a flawless ecosystem. Bira also becomes a spot for island hopping. Thanks to its nearby island.

The Nuance

Bira Island emits a wonderful nuance. The water has a flawless visibility. It astonishes any people who come to the island. The color of the water is green Tosca, actually. Near to the beach, you can see several cottages. Those become the best facilities on the island. In the island, there is a small pond. Your kids would definitely love it. Bira also features many trees. These create a cool and shady atmosphere. Thus, the island can be a perfect place for relaxing.

Exploring Bira Island

A tiring trip to Bira Island is worth an effort. At the end of your journey, you will be rewarded by beautiful nature and stunning nautical beauty. The best spot for sightseeing is on the dock. You can witness coral reefs and sea creatures from there. The water is clear so you can see those things visibly. Unlike its siblings, Harapan and Tidung Island, Bira is considered a resort island. There are villagers, so you can enjoy a peaceful holiday perfectly.

Diving is the most popular activity in Bira Island. Many professional divers often come there. The water visibility is excellent and the depth is moderate. It is a suitable for beginners, as well. Apart from diving, you can also enjoy snorkeling. As long as you have the gears, you are ready to go. If you don't like water sports, you can simply sit on the deck while feeding the fishes. It is a comfortable activity. Everyone would love it. On top of that, the fishes are attractive.

When it comes to facilities, Bira Island provides several cottages. You can rent a room and enjoy your solemn holiday there. In the afternoon, you can enjoy stunning views of the sunset. The breezy wind will be your companion. At night, you can stargaze and enjoy a nonviolent nuance. What's more? Sea urchins are common in Bira. Make sure you don't touch them. Even though they are unique, they can cause harm to you.

Nearby Attractions

- Macan Island
- Putri Island Beach
- Tidung Lagoon

How to Get There

Bira Island is located a little bit far from Jakarta. If you want a fast and comfortable trip, you should take a speedboat. This kind of service is available in Marina Ancol and the trip takes about 2 hours. If you use a local boat from Muara Angke, it takes longer which is 3-4 hours. The boat takes about 10-15 people. It can be quite uncomfortable sometimes. When it comes to accommodations, you can rent Bira Resort or hotels in Jakarta.

Where to Stay

- Jakarta Airport Hotel
- Bira Resort
- Hotel Huswah
- FM7 Resort Hotel
- Hotel Orchardz

Bokor Island

Getting Closer to Nature in Bokor Island, Thousand Islands Regency

Travelers have many reasons in visiting particular tourist destinations. One of them is to enjoy nature. In Thousand Islands Regency, there is a good destination called Bokor Island. Actually, it is a natural wildlife sanctuary. Visitors are able to witness numerous of animals and plants in the island. The most popular attraction is crab-eating macaque. Such unique species of monkey is abundant in Bokor. No wonder, those primates may accompany you while exploring the island. Have no fear. They cause no harms to human.

The Nuance

A calm nuance is not the only feature in Bokor Island. It also holds beautiful shorelines. The sand is soft, so you can walk on it without footwear. Not to mention the trees are shady and big. These create a comfortable nuance for tourists. Once you enter the forest, you may see several animals such as crab-eating macaques, birds, lizards, etc. If you are lucky, you can see hawksbill sea turtles in the seashore. Here is the thing. Bokor is situated near to Rambut Island. Thus, it is common seeing many species of birds there.

Exploring Bokor Island

As mentioned earlier, the main attraction in the island is its exotic animals. Though, you can also enjoy its numerous plants. These include mangroves, melinjo, ketapan, etc. On those trees, you can see several birds. Usually, they come from Rambut Island. With all these attractions, you should carry a camera. Many objects are available to capture! It is a waste if you don't take some pictures of them. If necessary, you must come with friends or families. This makes your vacation merrier.

Next fun activity is fishing. Bokor Island holds some good spots for those who love such hobby. Though, it takes a few minutes to reach them. One of the best fishing spots is Rumpon Beca. Using a boat, you can reach it within 15 minutes. The thing is you should have prepared a fish rod. For the best catches, you can use fresh squids or shrimps. Make sure to cut them first! Also, it is better to come with local people. They may teach you about an efficient way of fishing.

Fishing and sightseeing are two primary activities in Bokor Island. What is next? It is island hopping. Bokor is near to some islands, especially Rambut. Thus, visiting nearby islands is a good idea. That means you must prepare more money for a speedboat. The price goes up on holidays, though. If you want a cheaper price, you should come in working days instead. Don't forget to visit Untung Jawa Island, too!

Nearby Attractions

- Untung Jawa Island
- Lancang Island
- Rambut Island

How to Get There

It is easy to reach Bokor Island. What you need is a good boat either in Tanjung Pasir or Muara Angke. The trip takes longer if you come from Muara Angke, though. Once you have arrived at your destination, you can explore the island freely. Here is the thing. There are no accommodations. If you are looking for a hotel or resort, it is only available in more crowded islands like Untung Jawa.

Where to Stay

- Untung Jawa Resort

Cangkir Island

Cangkir Island in Thousand Islands Regency, Jakarta Indonesia never disappoints tourists. It is rich in islands. If you are visiting "Kepulauan Seribu", there is a recommended isle called Cangkir. Another name is Cangkir Kronjo. Why is called that way? Cangkir means "cup". It is because the island has a similar shape to such item. Apart from its unique shape, the island holds numerous attractions. Tourists keep coming due to different reasons. For instance, they want to visit a sacred tombstone. It is the resting place of a theologian of Banten.

The Nuance

The island is situated in the north part of Tangerang. The size is about 4.5 hectares. The thing is you can reach Cangkir easily. Thanks to the bridge. Visitors are able to cross the sea without hassles. It was an important project. This way, everyone can conduct a pilgrimage effortlessly there. The bridge is quite traditional. Even though it seems fragile, it is durable. In some occasions, you may encounter several fishers on it. When it comes to the best time to visit Cangkir, it is either during sunset or sunrise.

Exploring Cangkir Island

As mentioned before, most of the tourists come to the island for a pilgrimage. The gravestone belongs to Prince Jaga Lautan. He's the descendant of the first Banten Sultan. That means he's the son of Hasanudin. Before visiting such sacred burial site, you must know one thing. It takes some money to enter the location. That means you should pay both parking and entry fee. No worries. It is worth your money. Such pilgrimage gives you an amazing experience. It may replenish your spiritual level. Some tourists even look for blessings there.

Next thing to do in Cangkir Island is fishing. You are able to fish either on a deck or a boat. This activity is popular for those who look for a peaceful mood. One thing, tourists should carry their own rod. It is because you can't find any services in the isle. If you don't like fishing, you can simply buy fresh fishes from an auction location. It is situated near to the island. If you are good at bargaining, you can get cheap prices of good products!

Another fun activity is sightseeing. Some local fishermen are seen in the sea. Tourists are allowed to observe such activity freely. It is quite a sight. Apart from those natives, there are other attractive objects. For instance, there are mangroves. In Cangkir Island, you can also find several souvenir stores. Not to mention there are local "warungs". It is an opportunity to buy good stuff and eat delicious local foods. Thus, bringing more money is a good idea.

Nearby Attractions

- Tjo Soe Kong Monastery
- Pintu Seribu Mosque
- Tanjung Kait Beach

How to Get There

In order to reach Cangkir Island, you can depart either from Tangerang or Jakarta. Still, the fastest is from Tangerang. You don't even need to use a boat since there is a bridge connecting Java Island and Cangkir. It is a short and comfortable trip, for sure.

Where to Stay

- Hotel Santika BSD City Serpong
- Aston Paramount Serpong Hotel
- Kinari Residence

Cemara Kasih Kasih Beach

Cemara Kasih Kasih Beach in Tidung Island, Thousand Islands Regency

A great vacation should involve both a good location and a stunning atmosphere. In this case, you can find many of them in Thousand Islands Regency. In Tidung Island, there is a recommended beach called Cemara Kasih. Cemara means "pines" and Kasih means "love". Tourists are able to enjoy a flawless beauty and a refreshing atmosphere there. The beach is suitable for relaxation, hanging out, playing water, and family outing. The location is the west part of Tidung Island. Have no fear. It is easy to reach.

The Nuance

Once you reach the beach, you can feel a serene atmosphere. It is because the beach doesn't have many visitors, especially during workdays. In the seashore, you can find several trees. The best location for relaxation is definitely under those trees. The beach also features several facilities. These include a toilet and a coffee shop. That means you can hang out in such "warung" while enjoying breezy wind of the beach. There is also a homestay. It provides excellent accommodations and numerous amenities. This includes bikes for rent.

Exploring Cemara Kasih Kasih Beach

What can tourists do in Cemara Kasih Beach? Most of them love cycling. That doesn't mean you should carry your own bike. The resort provides it for you. What you need is to pay the rent fee. Riding a bicycle on the beach offers a different experience. One thing, the route isn't as smooth as that of the pavement. Still, you can enjoy it well. A beach roach is free from traffic. That means you can go freely without hassles. The breeze of the wind makes it more comfortable, too.

Next thing to do is playing on the seashore. The beach is suitable for a family outing. Have you ever played a cup castle? It is simple. You need only to build a structure from beach sand. Somehow, it improves your creativity and fun. Your kids will definitely love it. Beach bowling is also a good idea. Make some holes in the sand. Make sure they come in different size, though. Let your kids get points by throwing balls on those holes!

Once you have enjoyed all those activities, it is time to relax and drink coffee in the cottage. This is an ideal activity to end your day. With sea scenery and good nuance, you won't forget that moment. It can be romantic if you come with your spouse, for sure. As an alternative, you can visit some coffee stands near to the beach. After all, they offer better views that those of the cottages. Not to mention the prices are affordable.

Nearby Attractions

- Payung Island
- Kongsi Island
- Pari Island

How to Get There

The question is how you can get to Cemara Kasih Beach. It is a simple trip. From Muara Angke, take a local boat to Tidung Island. The trip takes faster if you depart from Marina Ancol with a speedboat, though. Once you reach the island, you can directly head to the homestay. Rent a room and take a rest for a while. Next, you can head to the beach and enjoy some activities there. It is going to be a wonderful vacation!

Where to Stay

➢ Cemara Kasih Homestay

Cipir Island

An Adventure in Cipir Island, Jakarta
In the Thousand Islands Regency, you can find Cipir Island. Another name is Khayangan Island. Some people also call it Kuipir Island. Today, it becomes a great location for a vacation in holidays or weekends. It is a suitable destination both for backpackers and travel addicts. It is located near to other islands, so you can explore them all within a single day. All of the islands hold historical values, as well. If you are looking for a distinct adventure, Cipir is highly recommended.

The Nuance

Once you have arrived at Cipir Island, you can see some dry trees. Brownish leaves create a rustic nuance there. In the beach, there are several buildings. These are quite old and emit unique atmosphere. In the afternoon, the island becomes more thrilling. You can hear several strange sounds there. Due to this reason, some people come here for an adventure. Not to mention the location is reachable. Many speedboats and ferries are available. On top of that, the transport fee is affordable.

Exploring Cipir Island

Cipir Island is part of "Kepulauan Seribu". So, what makes it special? First, it is the journey. In order to reach the island, you should conduct a tiring trip. Despite that fact, you are going to have a beautiful journey. Once you are reaching Muara Kamal, you can smell the fishy aroma. It is common. That port becomes your first checkpoint. That means you are ready to cross the sea and visit Cipir. A local fisherman's boat is sufficient. You can reach the island safely.

Once you reach Cipir Island, you can feel warm nuance. The atmosphere is a little bit cloudy, though. The island consists of many historical values. It is an ideal location for archeologists.

Those who love history would love it as well. In Cipir, there is a famous site called "Cipir Archeological Park. It is situated in the tip of the dock. Many old hospital structures are scattered around the island. Shady trees cover those structures. This creates an amazing nuance!

For those who love fishing, Cipir Island offers some great spots to catch fishes. The heat of the sun doesn't even matter. Another unique attraction is the broken bridge. It is located in a particular corner of the island. The bridge was used to evacuate the pilgrims from Onrust to Cipir. Why was that? Those people were infected by zymotic. In order to avoid the spread of the disease, these people were transformed to other location.

Nearby Attractions

- Onrust Island
- Kelor Island

How to Get There

If you come from Jakarta, you should visit Muara Angke. From here, you can continue your trip using a boat to Kelor Island. It is your checkpoint, after all. From Kelor, you can head to Cipir Island using another boat. It takes 40 minutes. The whole trip usually takes 3 hours. It can be faster if you choose a speedboat instead of a traditional boat. Also, make sure that you come in the right season. It is because rainy and windy weather makes your trip longer.

Where to Stay

- Mutiara Tidung
- Pantara Resort
- Tidung Lagoon

Damar Besar Island

Damar Besar Island and Its Majestic Lighthouse
Thousand Islands Regency is located in the north of Jakarta. In order to reach those islands, you should use a boat for sure. As for a reference, Damar Besar Island is a worthy destination. It is part of such archipelago. The name derives from Damar tree. No wonder, the island is covered by lots of such trees. For your information, there is another name of the isle. The locals call it Edam. Near to it, there is Damar Kecil Island. It has a smaller size and it is called Monyet Island.

The Nuance

It is easy to describe Damar Besar Island. Once you have arrived at the location, you may encounter lots of Damar trees. The beach is sloping and it features soft sand. When it comes to the water, it is calm. In fact, there are no waves near to the shorelines. This condition makes a perfect vacation destination. Another feature in the island is a majestic lighthouse. It becomes an icon there. Also, it becomes the main attraction. The views are indeed stunning from above!

Exploring Damar Besar Island

Many tourists come to the island to enjoy its historical value. Why? The island holds an ancient burial site. It belongs to Queen of Banten. No wonder, it becomes a perfect location for pilgrimage. The size of the cemetery is about 4x6 meters. Actually, there are 4 gravestones. As mentioned earlier, one of the tombstones belongs to Syarifah Fatimah. She was the Queen of Banten Sultanate. This woman came from Arab and became a ruler in Banten. The best time to visit is at noon. There is no light at night, so it is better not to come in the evening.

Once you explore such burial site, it is time to visit a grand lighthouse. The name is Vast Licht. It was a heritage of the Dutch Era. Despite its age, it keeps functioning as the guide for incoming boats. The height of the lighthouse is 65 meters. This structure was built in 1879. There is a keeper inside, so you can approach him and ask for permission. Your goal is to reach the top of the lighthouse. That is the spot for perfect scenery. Also, it becomes an attractive object for photography.

Damar Besar Island is uninhabited. That means you may expect a peaceful ambiance there. Also, it is a place to relax. For those with lots of burdens, you can eradicate them all in Damar Besar. Another idea is a family vacation. Bring your kids there, so you can introduce a great lighthouse and a mystical burial site.

Nearby Attractions

- Ayer Island
- Tanjung Pasir Beach
- Monyet Island

How to Get There

In the morning, you should have arrived at Muara Kamal in Tanggerang. It is a meeting point, actually. From here, you are going to ride a boat to Damar Besar Island. You depart along with other passengers. At least, there are 10 people in the boat. The cost of a boat ride depends on of seasons. In holidays, it may fluctuate significantly. In this case, make sure to come in the workdays. It doesn't matter if you bring lots of cash, though.

Where to Stay

- Ozone Hotel
- FM7 Resort

Dolphin Island

An Adventure in Dolphin Island, Thousand Islands Regency It is common knowledge. Thousand Islands consist of many islands. All of them are worth a visit, in fact. If you are looking for a reference, there is Dolphin Island. Why is the name? Dolphin means "Lumba-Lumba" in the Indonesian Language. Regardless of the name, there is no dolphin at all nearby. It is actually an uninhabited island. Also, it has an unspoiled beauty. Most tourists come there for camping and relaxation. If you want a new experience, you should visit the island.

The Nuance

Once you have arrived at the island, you can feel a solemn ambiance. It is because of its status. The island has no villagers. What you can get are an unspoiled beauty and a refreshing atmosphere. No wonder, it becomes an ideal location for camping. In the beach, you can see nearby islands from afar. There are some parts of shallow water, as well. In the back, you can find shady trees. The sky is clear and blue. It is reflected well on the sea surface.

Exploring Dolphin Island

As mentioned before, the island is suitable for camping. The thing is you should carry your own tent and camping equipment. Once you reach the island, it is time to build the tent. Make sure to build it under a tree. It helps create a comfortable and cool nuance. Make sure to build it before night. Thus, you can rest immediately. A trip to the island indeed is tiring. You need to replenish your stamina prior to doing some fun activities in the next day.

In the morning, it is time to explore the beach. It has a stunning underwater view. Don't be careless, though. There are many sea urchins nearby. If you look for more beautiful spots, there is Gosong Island. That means you must rent a boat to reach the island. It is only an accumulation of white sand. You can visit it during the low tide. Also, don't forget to carry a camera. Many beautiful objects are ready to capture. Make sure to take picture of them!

In the afternoon, you should go back to your tent. For further fun activities, there is a sunset! Sitting on the seashore and enjoying a beautiful sunset are good ideas. Lastly, you can enjoy BBQ at night. That means you have already prepared some fishes and meat beforehand. No worries, you can buy them in Harapan Island, which is your checkpoint in visiting Dolphin Isle. For a merrier nuance, a group vacation is recommended. That means you should come either with families or friends.

Nearby Attractions

- Gosong Island
- Harapan Island

How to Get There

It is easy to reach Dolphin Island. First, you should head to Muara Angke. From here, you must visit the checkpoint. It is in Harapan Island. Once you reach Harapan, there are some local boats to use. They are cheap and affordable. Still, you should prepare enough money, especially for next adventures like island hopping. If you come with your family, you are going to spend more money on your vacation.

Where to Stay

- Camping

Genteng Island

Visiting Genteng Island in Thousand Islands Regency, Jakarta

In Thousand Islands Regency, there is an island called Genteng. It is actually a small isle. The size is only 6 hectares. Despite the size, the island consists of a cottage and it becomes a recommended place for relaxation. The thing is Genteng is considered a private island. Still, it becomes a destination for a gathering and tour group. It is also possible to conduct either a wedding or private party there. Thanks to its exotic seawater and stunning sand. In a nutshell, it has an outstanding quality in terms of privacy and beauty.

The Nuance

The first impression is its remote nuance. Despite its small size, the island features numerous types of beauty. For instance, there is a paved pier. It has no fence, but it seems sturdy. From here, tourists can sit and enjoy the sea scenery. Near to it, there is a wooden structure. It is the keeper's den. In the beach, you may encounter soft and comfortable sand. In the back, there are some benches for tourists. Such location is covered by dense trees, so you can feel the refreshing mood.

Exploring Genteng Island

The most recommended activity in Genteng Island is snorkeling. One thing, there are no local services. That means you should carry your own gears. A life jacket is a must. The other important items are fins and goggles. It requires swimming skills, as well. Once you are in the water, you are able to witness beautiful fishes and coral reefs. Make sure not to ruin the reefs, though. If you don't like snorkeling, you can do other water sports. For example, there is a banana boat. Your kids would love it, for sure.

Genteng Island is a private land. Thus, you should not expect villagers. In terms of facilities, you can find many of them. The best one is a formation of cottages. At night, the guests are allowed to sing wholeheartedly in the karaoke room. Isn't that great? Unfortunately, Genteng is not as popular as Tidung or other islands in "Kepulauan Seribu". It lacks in marketing and exposure, after all. Not to mention it is a private island. It belongs to a grandson of former vice president of Indonesia. In the past, no tourists were allowed to visit it.

Even though Genteng Island has been available for public these days, it can't accommodate too many people. The maximum number of visitors is 48 people. Most of them come to Genteng for a special event like a wedding ceremony or a corporation meeting. Regular tourists are allowed to come there, too.

Nearby Attractions

- Matahari Island
- Sepa Island
- Putri Island

How to Get There

If you come from Jakarta, you can take a traditional motor boat in Muara Kamal. It takes much time, indeed. As an alternative, you can depart from Tanjung Kait in Tangerang. There is another way to reach Genting Island. It is from Marina Ancol. From here, you can use a speedboat. The trip is faster that way. Though, the price is more expensive than an old-fashioned motorboat. Are you ready to fund it?

Where to Stay

- Genteng Homestay

Gosong Rengat Island

Gosong Rengat Island in Thousand Islands Regency, Jakarta

Gosong Rengat Island becomes a recommended place for travelers. This small island was formed by a formation of corals and other nautical items. It was the result of sedimentation. Despite its small size, it has a distinct charm. Tourists often visit it for a vacation retreat. Due to its unspoiled beauty, the island has been a perfect place for a honeymoon. It terms of location, it is near to Perak Island. That means you can visit both the islands in a single trip.

The Nuance

The first impression when reaching Gosong Rengat Island is the pure white sand. Also, shallow and clear seawater may amaze you. In the shorelines, you can see several umbrellas and benches. Some tourists use them for relaxation and sightseeing. In the horizon, you can witness luxury boats and a nearby island. It feels like a paradise. During a nice weather, the wind blows comfortably. Even beach walking is not a bad idea. It is an opportunity to relax. Forget your works and god to Gosong instead.

Exploring Gosong Rengat Island

The locals have a unique story regarding the island, especially about its name. Gosong means "burned". In the past, many people sunbathed in the shorelines. Their body turned dark due to sun exposure. Today, the island has been visited by many tourists. Thanks to its flawless beauty. One thing, you should come in the right time. The island only occurs during the low tide. That means the land may disappear during the high tide.

Have no fear. Your tourist agent helps you to choose the right time in reaching Gosong.

Next thing to do is snorkeling. As mentioned before, the seawater is quite clear. The visibility is great as well. Even beginners can enjoy a wonderful nautical adventure in Rengat. Once again, you should take advantage of a tour guide. He or she helps you reach the best spots for snorkeling. It is better than wandering around alone. Also, make sure to come with friends or families. A companion makes your trip merrier. It doesn't have to be your friends, families are recommended, too.

Gosong Rengat Island is also suitable for photography. During the low tide, many beautiful objects are seen. It is a perfect time to enact an umbrella and a chair. You can sit and relax while watching sea scenery. However, you should not spend too long in Rengat. The heat of the sun may burn your skin and the high tide may ruin the land. Usually, tourists only spend a few hours in Gosong. Later, they visit nearby islands for more attractions.

Nearby Attractions

- Perak Island
- Melinjo Island

How to Get There

Here is the fact. Gosong Rengat Island is located in the northernmost of "Kepulauan Seribu". That means the trip takes the longest as compared to others. The location is near to Perak and Melinjo Island. From Tanjung Bait, you can use a speedboat to head to the island. It is faster than a traditional boat in Muara Angke. When it comes to accommodations, you should look for cottages in other islands. There are no facilities in Rengat, as well.

Where to Stay

- No hotels or cottages

Harapan Island

A Splendid Vacation in Harapan Island, Jakarta

Have you heard about Harapan Island? People also call it Hope Island. Due to its untouched beauty, the island becomes more popular these days. It is an ideal place for leisure. Also, it is a peaceful tourist spot for families. Even foreigners often come there! The island has featured numerous facilities. The most comfortable one is the homestay. You can rent it near to the port. Once you enjoy your breakfast, you are allowed to explore the island in the next morning!

The Nuance

First things come first. Travelers are looking for a peaceful nuance in Harapan Island. As the name implies, it is an island of inspiration and hope. It is likely you can eradicate all of your burdens there. The stunning views of the sea may astonish you. In the horizon, you can see green hills and trees. In the beach, there is a fenced pier. It has the shape of T letter, too. Isn't that unique? Some old boats are scattered on the shorelines. They become great extras in Harapan.

Exploring Harapan Island

Just like other islands in "Kepulauan Seribu", Harapan Island is a suitable area for snorkeling. No worries. Even beginners can enjoy such activity. It is because you can find an instructor and tour guide nearby. He or she has reliable experiences. Apart from snorkeling, you can conduct island hopping. That means you are going to visit nearby small islands using a boat. Those isles are uninhabited. They are quite peaceful and stunning. This is going to be an exotic vacation. Don't you think so?

Harapan Island is good for water sports. Tourists can enjoy numerous activities like riding a sofa boat, jet skiing, riding a banana boat, canoeing, etc. You must have a good stamina since there are many things to do later. In order to replenish your energy, you should relax in a nearby homestay. It features comfortable and high-quality amenities. The management has fulfilled the standards, after all. Each room is equipped with the best entertainment and comfortable furniture. When it comes to facilities, the island provides a police post, health services, places for praying, etc.

Here is the thing. Harapan Island doesn't support wireless connection and cellular signal. Is it a bad thing? No worries. A vacation in Harapan is going to be peaceful. It is an opportunity to disconnect from busy life. That means you don't even need to use your phone! What you need are beautiful nature and comfortable atmosphere. It is better to come with families or friends, though.

Nearby Attractions

- Macan Island
- Putri Island Beach
- Tidung Lagoon

How to Get There

It is a no brainer. In order to reach Harapan Island, your first destination is Muara Angke. It is the place to find a traditional boat. One thing, the location is smelly so you must bear it well. The trip takes about 4 hours. Not to mention you should gather first at the meeting point. If you want a more comfortable trip, you should more for it. For instance, there is a speedboat service in Ancol.

Where to Stay

- Jakarta Airport Hotel
- Harapan Homestay
- Hotel Huswah
- FM7 Resort Hotel
- Hotel Orchardz

Hawksbill Sea Turtle Conservation

Visiting Hawksbill Sea Turtle Conservation in Tidung Island Tidung Island is indeed a beautiful place for a vacation. It is part of "Kepulauan Seribu". The location is near to Jakarta! The island holds numerous tourist attractions, too. One of them is conservation for hawksbill sea turtle. Despite its small size, the location is considered attractive. Many tourists visit it for witnessing such cute creatures. Are you interested? In this case, you can come with your family. The kids would definitely love them. With an authorization, visitors are allowed to hold the turtles.

The Nuance

As mentioned before, the size of the building isn't big. There are several ponds there. Each of them contains dozens of small turtles. They are cute! Their appearance is unique. Their mouth is curved and their skin has the texture of a chainsaw. A unique part is the color of their shell. It may alter into different color depending on water temperature. The conservation area offers a shady nuance. Thus, it is comfortable for visitors. Also, you can introduce such species to your kids. It will be a worthy education.

Exploring Hawksbill Sea Turtle Conservation

It is a no brainer. The main attraction in the conservation is definitely the turtles. Hawksbill sea turtles are considered an endangered species. In Indonesia, there are no more than 500. Tourists can learn about the history of such species and its threats. One of the biggest threats is human. People keep hunting it illegally. By learning the story, you are able to contribute to the conservation project. At least, you won't do bad things to nature. Not to mention you can teach your kids regarding the importance of conservation.

Next thing to do in hawksbill sea turtle conservation is an observation. That means tourists are allowed to witness how to take care of the turtles. The keeper may show you how to do it. Due to this reason, it is better to carry a camera. Those turtles are indeed cute and beautiful. Thus, you should not miss an opportunity to take some pictures of them. Selfies are allowed. Though, make sure not to cause havocs in the location. Otherwise, the keeper may send you away.

Another fun activity is watching the release of "tukik". It is the name of ready-to-an-adventure turtles. Those small sea turtles will be released in the open sea when reaching an appropriate age. It is indeed an interesting sight. The thing is you should come in the right time. It is because the keeper doesn't do it every time. If you are lucky, you can witness them. If not, you should gather information regarding when the release of those sea turtles is.

Nearby Attractions

- Jembatan Cinta
- Perawan Beach
- Shark Conservation

How to Get There

Are you visiting Tidung Island in the near future? In this case, what you need is the right transportation. From Jakarta, head to Muara Angke. It is the place to rent a motorboat. Next, your destination is Tidung. The trip is about 2 hours. Once you reach the island, you can directly head to the conservation area. It takes only a few minutes, actually.

Where to Stay

- Cottage Anggrek 3
- Tidung Lagoon
- Tidung Citra

Jukung Island

Jukung Island in Thousand Islands Regency, Jakarta

Do you have a plan in visiting Thousand Islands Regency? In this case, what you need is a destination. For instance, there is Jukung Island. Another name is Ayu Besar Island. However, it is not considered as major islands in "Kepulauan Seribu". Still, it is a worthy vacation destination for you. Tourists recognize it as a natural conservation for birds. The most popular ones are osprey and white-bellied sea eagle. Those species are attractive. In fact, they become the main attraction on the island.

The Nuance

Jukung Island is uninhabited. Once you have arrived on the island, there are no people at all. What you can find are trees and wild animals. A shady environment is indeed astonishing. What's next? It is the beach. The sand is white and the sea is calm. Apart from eagles, you can find other animals like crows, lizards, etc. In some parts of the island, there are mangroves, Casuarina equisetid folia, etc. Sometimes, people from nearby islands come there for harvesting nature resources. They come from Harapan and Kelapa Island. Though, it is a rare event.

Exploring Jukung Island

The location is near to other islands. That means you should explore other locations, too. Jukung Island is famous for its natural attractions. Though, it lacks in facilities. In this case, you can obtain good accommodations and facilities in other islands. Despite its weakness, Jukung has been included in the best list of vacation destinations. Not to mention it is a free land. Everyone is allowed to enter it. No fees are included, at all. It is a perfect location for exploring nature!

Next adventure is in the sea. Jukung Island also has a nautical beauty. It features colorful and abundant corals. Thus, you can perform either snorkeling or diving. Since there are no facilities, you should have prepared your snorkeling gear. For beginners, it is better to come with friends. Hiring an instructor is also recommended. He or she helps becomes your guide to explore the beautiful underwater. For the best experience, you must wear high quality gears. Those provide more comfortable and safer performance, indeed.

The island is the home of several species of eagles. In this case, bringing a camera is a must. It gives you an opportunity to capture beautiful creatures and objects. Another thing to do is island hopping. Make sure to rent a boat for a day. You are going to use it later. Not only the boat, but you are going to hire a navigator. He knows the route to nearby islands. No wonder, you should depend on him much. Thus, don't forget to give him some tips.

Nearby Attractions

- Kelor Island
- Hantu Island
- Matahari Island

How to Get There

How can you get there? Muara Angke is your first point. It is an ideal location to find good boats. Don't forget to hire a navigator! Thus, you should have prepared more money. Another location to find a boat is in Marina Ancol. What makes it different? You can find better boats there, which are faster and more comfortable.

Where to Stay

➢ No hotels

Kelapa Island

A Soothing Vacation in Kelapa Island, Thousand Islands Regency
If you are visiting Thousand Islands Regency, you should never miss Kelapa Island. In terms of beauty, it is the same as Tidung's. Moreover, it offers a solemn ambiance. Kelapa is inhabited by up to 5,200 villagers. The size of the island is about 13.10 hectares. As the name suggests, you can find many coconut trees on it. Kelapa means "coconut". It is also located near to other islands like Kotok, Kaliage, and Harapan Island. Thus, it is possible to perform an island hopping tour from here.

The Nuance

The sea is quite calm and deep. You won't see wild waves there. In the beach, you can see soft and white sand. There are several wooden huts in the shorelines. Behind, you may see numerous coconut trees. They are quite tall. Also, some bushes and trees are covered the island. For those who look for a great spot for relaxation, the seashore in Kelapa Island is a recommended choice. In the sea, you can see some fish traps. In some occasions, you can see fishermen.

Exploring Kelapa Island

Once you reach Kelapa Island, you can explore it using local vehicles. "Becak" is quite common there. Not to mention the fee is affordable. When it comes to the best tourist destination, it is definitely the beach. Most of the visitors love to play sand. It is due to its soft and beautiful texture. With this in mind, you should come with your kids. It is an opportunity for a family vacation, so you can create a sand castle together.

There are different tour packages in Kelapa Island. You can choose one based on your budget. An island hopping is a must, so you should have prepared money for it. In the east part of the island, it is a route to Harapan Island. You don't even need to use a boat to reach it. Both the islands are connected with a land path. If you want to spend more than one day in Kelapa, you must look for a local inn. No worries, the options are many.

In the afternoon, you can enjoy the sunset. The best spot to enjoy it is on the beach. Make sure to come back to your room before midnight! In the next morning, you should try snorkeling. You can rent the gears in Forestry Ministry Office. They provide it for tourists, after all. Not to mention they have a complete option of snorkeling gears. What's next? Campers often visit the island. It is because some spots of the island are suitable for camping. Make sure to bring the equipment, though.

Nearby Attractions

- Opak Island
- Harapan Island
- Kaliage Island
- Kotok Island

How to Get There

If you come from Muara Angke, it takes about 3.5 hours. A traditional motor boat takes longer than a speedboat, after all. From the port, you should head north and pass through Pramuka Island. Once you reach Kelapa Island, you won't see many tourists. Most of the people are villagers. Also, don't forget to rent a room first. Later, you can explore the island passionately.

Where to Stay

➤ Kelapa Inns

Kaliage Island

A Private Resort in Thousand Islands Regency - Kaliage
Many islands are scattered in Thousand Islands Regency. They are all part of Jakarta, though. If you are visiting such small archipelago, make sure to come to Kaliage Island. It is famous for its luxurious resort. It belongs to a typhoon named Surya Paloh. Despite its status, the island is open for public. That means tourists are allowed to enjoy their holidays there. One thing, it is definitely pricier than other resorts in "Kepulauan Seribu". Due to this reason, you must carry lots of cash.

The Nuance

In terms of appearance, Kaliage Island is similar to nearby islands. It features dense trees and beautiful sea. The thing is it has a tower. It functions as a signal receiver, so the guests can browse the internet and enjoy entertainment in a maximum way. There are several cottages near to the beach. That means you can relax inside while witnessing gorgeous scenery out there. Some parts of sea water are clear and shallow. It becomes an unavoidable temptation. Almost all visitors would like to enjoy water sports in Kaliage.

Exploring Kaliage Island

The island is uninhabited. There are only some villas and cottages scattered around Kaliage Island. There are some keepers, though. Even though it is open for public, you should get permission in entering the island. Despite this problem, you won't get bored in Kaliage. You can meet other visitors, as well. Mostly, they come from Jakarta. It is a no brainer. They are rich people! What they want are luxury and privacy. What about you? You should try it at least once!

Apart from a flawless beach, Kaliage Island has other attractions. For many, the best one is Isle East Indies Resort. It is located in small Kaliage Isle. The thing is it becomes one of the most recommended places to stay in Thousand Islands Regency. It is suitable either for couples or families. The resort is surrounded by trees, so it gives a comfortable sensation. Each of the rooms applies a traditional architecture. It combines Indonesian and colonialism designs. The rooms represent Indonesian's culture, after all. You can feel a distinct nuance.

In front of your room, there is vast white sand. From there, you can witness beautiful sea scenery. It will be an amazing experience for you. In the next morning, you can enjoy numerous water sports like canoeing, snorkeling, diving, swimming, and much more. For those who love snorkeling, the best spot to reach is the left part of the island. Don't forget to eat your breakfast first. The resort provides it freely in the morning. It is one of the amenities, after all.

Nearby Attractions

- Kelapa Island
- Opak Island
- Harapan Island

How to Get There

The location is a little bit far from Jakarta. Mostly, tourists may depart from Muara Angke. The most common transportation is traditional motor boats. If you look for a more comfortable trip, there are speedboats in Marina Ancol. They cost more than regular boats but offer great comfort and efficacy. No worries. It is worth your money. The trip becomes simpler, as well.

Where to Stay

- Isle East Indies

Karang Island

Visiting Karang Island in Thousand Islands Regency, Jakarta

Kepulauan Seribu" holds many beautiful isles. One of the islands is called Karang. The location is near to Pramuka Island. Most of the tourists visit it for a vacation retreat and snorkeling, actually. For many, Karang is considered a romantic place. It is secluded and mysterious. Despite its thrilling atmosphere, it holds many beautiful objects and spots. You can do many things there. These include snorkeling, trekking, and photography. Island hopping is a good idea, too. It is because Karang is situated near to neighboring islands.

The Nuance

Karang Island only has one flaw. It is the inexistence of a pier. Thus, you may expect wet clothes when reaching the land. Due to this reason, make sure to carry extra clothes. The sea water has the color of light green. It looks beautiful indeed. Once you reach the island, you can see a small house. It looks old and unmaintained. However, it is a home of the keeper. The house is surrounded by tall trees. What a stunning view! It looks like a deserted home on an uninhabited island.

Exploring Karang Island

In a nutshell, Karang Island is a perfect location for relaxation. It features natural beauty and solemn mood. For many, an island is an ideal place for a family vacation. Why is that? They can retreat from daily routines and spend quality times with their beloved ones. Also, snorkeling is possible. The thing is you should not expect beautiful coral reefs. Some visitors have ruined them carelessly. As an alternative, you can fish. For those who have prepared a fishing rod, the beach has some spots for fishing!

Your next activity is camping. Karang Island becomes a good spot for those who love nature. The best location is in Karang Congkak. It is a small island located near to the main island. One thing, you should spend about 3 hours to reach it. There are no people living there. Not to mention you can't find facilities. With these in mind, you must prepare refreshments and proper equipment. The trees grow wild and there are no lights. At night, you only depend on your bonfire.

In the morning, you should have gone back to the main island. Before going back to Java Island, you should take your time witnessing sea scenery once again. The sound of the waves and breezy wind create an unforgettable mood. If you are lucky, you can see several Java Eagles. They live in Karang Island and nearby islands. As a final adventure, you can do island hopping. Some nearby islands are worth to visit, after all.

Nearby Attractions

- Semak Daun
- Pramuka Island

How to Get There

From Muara Angke, a traditional motor boat may take you to Pramuka Island. From there, you can head to Karang Island using another boat. It is not a long trip, but you it seems uncomfortable due to big waves. For a faster trip, a speedboat is a better but pricier option. You can have one in Marina Ancol.

Where to Stay

- Aston Marina Hotel
- Resorts in Untung Jawa
- Putri Duyung Ancol Hotel
- Mercure Convention Centre Ancol Hotel

Karya Island

Karya Island and the Chinese Culture, Thousand Islands Regency
You should know Thousand Islands Regency is part of Jakarta. This archipelago on which tourists often visit is indeed

interesting. One of them is Karya Island. The locals also call it Cina Island. Cina means Chinese. No wonder, you can find many reminiscences of Chinese (Tionghoa) culture in the island. Some researchers have found several ceramics around the sea and land. Apart from that, the island offers a stunning beauty. Also, this small island has attracted both domestics and foreign tourists every year.

The Nuance

Karya Island is located near to Panggang Island. People from Panggang take advantage of Cina Island as a burial site. Some people from Pramuka Island also do the same thing. That means you may expect many gravestones in some parts of the island. Have no fear. Those create a unique sight. When it comes to attractions, the island becomes the home of many creatures such as crows, lizards, kepodang birds, and much more. What about the plants? Coconut and Sentigi trees are common there.

Exploring Karya Island

The first thing to do in Cina Island is sightseeing. Beautiful sea scenery is indeed captivating. It never fails to amaze visitors. The beach is tourists' favorite spot. It features beautiful white sand and clear sea water. Some ceramics and valuable items were found in the sea. The founders believed them were Chinese's. Here is the fact. They also found some bones having characteristics of Chinese in the water! These findings suggest there was a settlement back then. The people lived in the past were definitely Chinese.

In the midst of Karya Island, you can find a traditional settlement. It is the home of the natives. Most of them are Madura and Bugis tribes. They have been living there for years. Thus, you have an opportunity to learn their culture. A tour guide may help you to communicate with those people, after all. It will be better if you can talk a little bit "Bahasa Indonesia". The village is surrounded by shady trees. If you come at the beach, there are mangroves. Those plants protect the land from sea erosion.

A history of Cina Island is considered amusing. Many tourists come to the location for learning the past settlement in such mysterious land. It is said Chinese fled from Great Britain using some boats. They brought their valuable items with them. Unfortunately, they were struck by a deadly disease while passing "Kepulauan Seribu". According to locals, those people were looking for remedies in the island. Unluckily, the failed and died one at a time. You can learn this story from the natives, after all.

Nearby Attractions

- Panggang Island
- Semak Daun Island
- Pramuka Island

How to Get There

From Jakarta, you must head to Muara Angke. It is a meeting point, so tourists can depart using a traditional motor boat. The trip takes about 2 hours. Make sure you carry proper equipment, so your journey will be comfortable. For those who want a faster trip, you must head to Marina Ancol first. It is where you can find a speedboat service.

Where to Stay

- Hotels in Jakarta
- Cottages in Untung Jawa Island

Kelor Island

Visiting Antique Kelor Island in Jakarta

A Thousand Islands Regency offers many tourist spots. If you look for a reference, there is a recommended choice like Kelor Island.

In the past, people called it Kherkof Island. It is located near to Bidadari and Onrust Island. From Ancol Beach, the distance is only 1.9 km. No wonder, it had a similar function to those islands back then. In fact, there is a wreck of the Seventh Provincien. The ship was used to fight the Dutch. Unfortunately, it was destroyed and sank near to the island.

The Nuance

What you can enjoy in Kelor Island is its simplicity. The island offers chic nuance and plain seawater. It features several traditional piers. Those are made of bamboos. There are also several fishermen's boats near to those docks. Near to the beach, there is an ancient fort. It was the ruin of the Dutch Colonialism. One thing, there is no light on the island. At night, you may expect a chilling nuance for sure. Some people even consider it a creepy island.

Exploring Kelor Island

Despite its small size, the island holds a valuable history. You can find numerous heritages of the colonialism era. Apart from that, Kelor holds beautiful beach views. It is a perfect location for beach walking and sightseeing. In the sea, you may expect some people fishing. They are looking for groupers. If you love fishing, you can try it as well. Make sure to carry your own fishing rod, though. Also, it requires a permit. That means you should talk to the island keeper first prior to fishing in Kelor.

Next common thing to do is photography. Kelor Island becomes a suitable location for a pre-wedding photo session. The best backgrounds are the Dutch's Ruins. For the best results, you must use a good camera. Also, learn some photography skills. If not, you can hire a professional photographer. He has both experiences and skills to capture the best pictures. The thing is you must pay some fees. In some cases, you need to spend more than you have expected.

As for tips, it is better to carry some refreshments. These include the drinks and snacks. You are going to explore the island, so you must have prepared. An island hopping is also possible. It is because Kelor is located near to Cipir and Onrust. In fact, you can explore those islands within a single day. That means you don't even need an accommodation. Don't forget to carry a camera! Some objects in Kelor are worth a photo shoot.

Nearby Attractions

- Onrust Island
- Cipir Island

How to Get There

The most common transportation is a traditional boat. You can get this in Muara Angke. Actually, Kelor Island is part of a tour package. These include Onrust and Cipir Island. No wonder, you are able to visit those islands one at a time. They are located near to each other, as well. A trip to Kelor usually takes about 2-3 hours. It can be longer if you are trapped in bad weather. Due to this reason, make sure you have learned the schedule.

Where to Stay

- Mutiara Tidung
- Pantara Resort
- Tidung Lagoon

King Pandita's Tombstone

A Sacred Place in Tidung Island King Pandita's Tombstone Tidung Island is part of "Kepulauan Seribu". It is considered popular among travelers, as well. In small Tidung, there is a sacred tombstone of King Pandita. Usually, the tour agency may create a tour program for tourists. Thus, everyone can easily access such tourist spot. What about you? Are you interested? It is an interesting religious tourism, after all. When you are visiting

Tidung Island, you must never miss it. You can learn the story behind it and take some pictures of the tombstone.

The Nuance

There are actually 3 tombstones. Apart from King Pandita's gravestone, you can see two others. They belong to his relations. These tombstones are located in a small building. Thus, they come in a good condition. A keeper takes a good care of them, as well. Visitors are allowed to enter the house with an authorization. The color of the ceramics is pastel. Each of them has a wooden headstone. It has a shape of a mosque tower. Sometimes, visitors are seen inside the room. In this case, make sure not to step on the tombstones!

Exploring King Pandita's Tombstone

King Pandita's Tombstone is famous for its sacredness. No wonder, tourists come there for blessings. It also holds a good story. During the Dutch Colonialism, he was exiled by the invaders. Actually, Pandita has another name, it is Muhammad Kaca. He came from Malinau, East Kalimantan. His rebellion against imperialism made him a convict. He was sent to Tidung Island and died in 1898. Today, his tombstone becomes a significant lure in the island. As a tourist, you can learn his story from the locals.

Religious tourism becomes more popular these days. It helps people find serenity. Regardless of the reasons, more people keep coming to King Pandita's Tombstone. Usually, tourists want to learn the history of Muhammad Kaca. The keeper even tells visitors about it freely. Not only tourists, some historians take advantage the location for a research. Since the building is clean, you will be comfortable there. Also, visitors are allowed to take pictures inside the room. Isn't that great? Even though it is rare, tourists can take selfies.

One thing, all visitors should take care of the environment. That means you are not allowed to litter. If you want to eat snacks or drink something, you must go outside. At least, you must show respect to that place. It is a sacred tombstone, after all. Giving a prayer is not mandatory. However, most visitors do it. It is not likely you miss an opportunity to pray there. Somehow, the locals are considered the tombstone as a sacred thing. They believe it gives blessings to those who pray there.

Nearby Attractions

> Love Bridge

- Animal Conservation
- Tidung Nautical Garden

How to Get There

Your primary destination is Tidung Island. From Jakarta, you should visit Muara Angke. It is the place to rent a local motorboat. The trip takes about 2-3 hours. Once you reach the island, you need to head to Small Tidung Island by a bicycle. No worries. It takes only a few minutes to reach the tombstone.

Where to Stay

- Cottage Anggrek 3
- Tidung Lagoon
- Tidung Citra

Kongsi Island

Enjoying Good Times in Kongsi Island, Thousand Islands Regency

Here is the thing. Thousand Islands Regency offers lots of vacation destinations to travelers. If you are looking for a reference, there is Kongsi Island. It is located near to Pari Island, so you can visit both of them simultaneously. It consists of three different islands, which are West, Middle, and East Kongsi. All of them have similar characteristics and landscapes, actually. They also become the home of famous fauna called Brahminy kite. The locals call it BK. In fact, Kongsi becomes natural conservation of such majestic creature.

The Nuance

In terms of appearance, Kongsi Island is both beautiful and peaceful. It has similar seawater to other islands in "Kepulauan Seribu". The sea water is crystal clear, so it radiates mesmerizing beauty. Sometimes, some boats pass by on it. It is quite a view. During nice weather, the sky is reflected perfectly on the water. In the land, you can witness dense plants. When it comes to the beach, it features stunning white sand. Make sure you never miss island hopping.

Exploring Kongsi Island

As mentioned before, Kongsi Island is famous for its "Elang Bondol". Brahminy Kite has a moderate size. It is about 40-50 cm. The wings are wide and their tail is short. It is a unique type of an eagle, indeed. Their chest and necks are white. The rest of the head are reddish. Due to their uniqueness, the government decides to take care of such species in Kongsi. Today, more visitors want to reach natural conservation of Bondol Eagle and witness their cuteness directly.

Next adventure is snorkeling. It is both fun and challenging. Everyone is able to enjoy such activity, in fact. You are going to explore the nautical beauty of Kongsi Island. Many types fish swimming in it. Not to mention you can find stunning corals. It is recommended to carry an underwater camera. You won't miss those beautiful objects, will you? The thing is you must come either in the morning or afternoon. It helps you prevent the heat of the sun. Also, make sure to wear proper gears!

Another thing to do is island hopping. That means you visit nearby islands in a chorus. It takes both time and money, for sure. You must rent a good boat as well. Each of the islands features different characteristics. In Kongsi, there are mangroves and numerous exotic birds such as Bondol Eagle and black crows. There are other animals, though. These include forest rats and lizards. If you want to witness other creatures, you must visit Burung Island. No worries. It is near to Kongsi.

Nearby Attractions

- Pari Island
- Pasir Perawan Beach
- Burung Island

How to Get There

Your primary destination is Muara Angke. It is located in the north part of Jakarta. From here, you head to Kongsi Island using a traditional motor boat. No wonder, it takes a little bit longer than a speedboat. Though, the price is nice. For a better experience, you can take advantage of a powerboat. With more money, you can reach Kongsi comfortably.

Where to Stay

- Ibis Styles
- J Hotel
- FM7 Resort

Kresek Beach

A Vacation in Kresek Beach, Pari Island

If you are visiting Thousand Islands Regency, you must consider Pari Island. It is the home of numerous natural attractions. For instance, there is Kresek Beach. The name is derived from a banyan tree. The beach offers a solemn nature and soothing ambiance. You can do many things there such as beach walking, looking for clams, and enjoy sea scenery. The locals usually hang out at the beach and eat fries called toothless gum. The best thing is the environment. Kresek is the home of numerous trees. That means you can expect refreshing atmosphere there.

The Nuance

As mentioned before, Kresek Beach is surrounded by trees. Most of them are pines and coconut trees. They are shady and beautiful. In the shorelines, you may expect several granites. Despite this fact, the sand also becomes the part of the beach as well. When it comes to the sea, the waves are considered strong. In the horizon, you can see green hills. During the hot season, there isn't much cloud. That means you won't expect much rain, too. No worries. It is the best time to visit Kresek.

Exploring Kresek Beach

The thing is you aren't able to swim in the water. Thus, you should look for other activities. For instance, there is BBQ. You only need to gather ingredients and equipment. The locals also often visit this area for a family outing. During the holidays, you may expect lots of people in this location. They come different parts of Indonesia. Most of them come from Jakarta, though. At night, you can join them grilling some fishes and other ingredients. If you come with friends, you can make your own bonfire!

Your next adventure is in the sea. Kresek Beach has a moderate nautical beauty. Even though it isn't as good as in Tidung, tourists are able to see numerous sea creatures. These include hawksbill sea turtles, starfishes, sea urchins, mantas, and much more. The best attraction is the natural conservation for "penyu sisik". Foreigners call it hawksbill sea turtles. It is managed by the locals. Though, you should not expect superior facilities there. It helps you get along well with nature.

Overall, Kresek is indeed recommended. In the morning, you can play in the seashore. In the afternoon, you should visit sea turtle conservation. At night, tourists are able to enjoy BBQ. Here is the thing. You should pay the entry fee. No worries. It is cheap. The money is used by the locals to keep the beach clean and comfortable. Therefore, you may expect a flawless beauty of the beach. With this in mind, visitors should never litter.

Nearby Attractions

- Lancang Island
- Kongsi Island

How to Get There

Kresek Beach is located in Pari Island. From Muara Angke, you can directly head to Pari. It takes about 4-5 hours. If you look for a faster trip, you need to go to Marina Ancol. From here, there are several speedboats to rent. It is more comfortable but pricier. Thus, make sure to prepare your budget well.

Where to Stay

- Aco Homestay
- Dua putri Homestay
- Asrama LIPI
- Mole Pulau Pari
- Bahri Homestay
- Ibu Ibad

Laki Island

A Worthy Vacation in Laki Island, Thousand Islands Regency

"Kepulauan Seribu" becomes more popular over time. It is because tourists can find unlimited attractions in such archipelago. One of the best islands is called Laki. It is located near to Cangkir Island. Laki means "a man". There is no official record regarding the history of such name. Though, some people make a speculation. Laki Island was a base of VOC. There was a nightclub back then and it was filled only by men. There was no woman on the island, at all.

The Nuance

Despite its unclear history, Laki Island attracts tourists these days. It is because of its distinct beauty. There are Laki Besar and Laki Kecil. Both of them are stunning. In the estuary, the water is flawless and clear. It is calm, as well. No wonder, people come there for fishing. In the back, there are several shady plants. All of those features create a perfect nuance for hunting fishes. One thing, you must come during nice weather. Otherwise, there are no fishes nearby. Rain makes you uncomfortable as well.

Exploring Laki Island

Most tourists come to Laki Island for relaxation. Thanks to the presence of 15 bungalows. All of them feature great facilities such as a jogging track and swimming pools. The tracks are about 5 km and it surrounds the island. Thus, you can come with your family for a vacation retreat. For couples, Laki is also a perfect place for a honeymoon. You don't even need to carry lots of money. Still, you must consult with a tour agent first.

Fishing is also an interesting activity in Laki Island. Don't be surprised with the presence of numerous men in the seashore. According to some experienced fishermen, the island holds good spots for catching squids. Once you have caught several fishes and squids, you can even grill them directly on the spot. Due to this reason, you should have prepared the utensils. For merrier events, you should come with families or friends. A group tour is considered more valuable, after all.

Laki Island is uninhabited. A peaceful atmosphere hits you when you reach the island. With this, you can take advantage of its solemn nature. It helps you eradicate stresses and burdens. For busy people, the island becomes a natural resort. Despite its deserted status, Laki features a good homestay. Everyone has the same opportunity to enjoy its luxuries. What you need is money, so you can explore other islands, too. The most recommended island to visit after Laki is Cangkir Island. Make sure to put it on your list!

Nearby Attractions

- Tanjung Kait Beach
- Lancang Island
- Cangkir Island

How to Get There

The best place to depart is Mauk Beach. It is located in Sepatan, Tangerang. From here, you can take a speedboat to Laki Island. Approximately, the trip takes 25-30 minutes. Once you reach the island, you can either choose a camp site or a bungalow. Each of them offers different experience and nuance. If you don't come with lots of money, you should go camping.

Where to Stay

- FM7 Resort
- Ibis Styles
- J Hotel
- Laki Homestay

Lancang Island

Lancang Island and Its Traditional Ambiance

Real travelers look for new places to explore. Have you heard Thousand Islands Regency? It is part of Jakarta, actually. Many options of islands are available for tourists. Here is a reference. The name is Lancang Island. Some experienced travelers recommend it to newbies. Why is that? The island is suitable for finding peace and relaxation. It is because the government limits the use of motor vehicles on it. Thus, you may expect a fresh and pollution-free environment. Not to mention it features gorgeous scenery!

The Nuance

Lancang Island becomes a symbol of nature. It offers a solemn nuance and refreshing atmosphere. In the sea, you can find several fish traps. Those make distinct scenery, indeed. Not to mention the seawater is quite calm. For the best experience, you should visit the beach before sunset. At that time, you are able to witness the fall of the sun. It sets beautifully and emits a romantic atmosphere. The island also features several facilities. You can even find a majestic homestay there.

Exploring Lancang Island

The first reason to visit Lancang Island is the nature. You can do many things, especially on the beach. In fact, it costs almost nothing. Fishing is the most popular activity there. No wonder, you will see many local people swarming in the shorelines. They enjoy it much. If you want a more challenging activity, there is snorkeling. Thanks to a good visibility of the sea. What you need are snorkeling gears and some skills. With these, you are ready to go.

Snorkeling is a primary attraction in Lancang Island. Tourists love its affordable price, after all. It is even cheaper than other islands. Both beginners and pros are allowed to explore the sea. That doesn't mean you can carelessly enter the water. At least, you must learn the basics. A guide may tell you to get a dry snorkel. The best choice is the one that comes with a splash guard. It helps you get rid of seawater easily out of the tube

Next consideration is the fins. Make sure you get fins that fit. It has a significant impact on the comfort, actually. Moreover, it helps you move safely in the water. On the other hand, unfit fins often lead to troubles. With these things in mind, you can enjoy snorkeling in a safe manner. What's next? It is time to fill your belly. In the evening, the best activity is grilling fishes. BBQ is available in the homestay. On top of that, don't forget to try traditional sauces of Lancang Island!

Nearby Attractions

- Tanjung Kait Beach
- Pasir Perawan Beach
- Tanjung Pasir Beach
- Laki Island

How to Get There

In order to reach Lancang Island, you have two options. First, it is in Muara Angke Port. There is a popular sea transportation called Krapu. The price is nice and the condition is good. Make sure you come in the morning, so you won't miss the boat. Another choice is to Rawasaban Port. It is located in Tangerang. You can take a ferry from there.

Where to Stay

- Lancang Homestay
- J Hotel
- Orchardz Hotel
- Zest Hotel

Lipan Island

Lipan Island in Thousand Islands Regency, Jakarta
In the next holiday, you should consider Lipan Island. This is a stunning tourist destination. The location is near to Kelapa Island. Thus, it is suitable for an island hopping. It is an uninhabited island, actually. Due to its serenity, many tourists come there for relaxation. Lipan means "centipede". No one knows the story of the island, though. That doesn't mean you may encounter lots of centipedes there. Today, people only recognize it as a wonderful vacation destination. It is suitable for everyone regardless of the purposes of holidays.

The Nuance

In terms of appearance, Lipan Island is shady and solemn. It is surrounded by trees and several bushes. In the pier, you can find some structures. Once again, there are no inhabitants. There is only a couple living on the island. They are the keepers, actually. The sea has moderate waves and it is considered safe for swimming. During summer, the sky is so clear. It emits a comfortable ambiance. For those who are looking for a peace, Lipan should be on the list.

Exploring Lipan Island

Since there are inhabitants, you can explore the island wholeheartedly. Both the pier and villas are located in the south part of Lipan Island. Thus, you should choose that location for the best vacation spot. Once you reach the island, take a rest in your room first. Make sure to eat well before exploring the island. Thick trees and an unspoiled beauty become major attractions there. You are allowed to explore them with an authorization of the keeper. One thing, always wear proper footwear before walking around the island!

In some occasions, there are wild animals passing by. These include seagulls, lizards, crows, and eagles. They become a beautiful object for photography. Due to this reason, make sure to bring your camera! As an alternative, you must reach the pier. It is a good spot for selfies. In the afternoon, you should visit the pier again. At this time, you are going to enjoy a stunning sunset. It is quite romantic and calming. Make sure not to miss such opportunity!

At night, you should go back to your room. Eat some foods and take a rest. In the morning, you should have been in the pier before dawn. It gives you a flawless beauty of the sunrise. What a great view! This may replenish your soul right away. Before going back to Java Island, make sure to visit nearby islands first. An island hopping will be your last adventure in Lipan Island. A local boat may carry you to nearby isles, especially Kelapa Island. Enjoy!

Nearby Attractions

- Opak Island
- Harapan Island

How to Get There

Everyone can reach Lipan Island easily. It only takes about 4 hours from Jakarta. Your meeting point is Muara Angke. From there, you must take a local boat to your destination. For those who are looking for a faster trip. There is Marina Ancol. From there, you can take a speedboat. It is more comfortable but expensive. No worries. It is worth an expense.

Where to Stay

- Lipan Villas

Macan Island

A Vacation Retreat to Macan Island in Thousand Islands Regency, Jakarta

"Kepulauan Seribu" is the home of stunning islands. One of them is Macan Island. Another name is Tiger Island. Are there many tigers in it? Have no fear. It is only a name. No one knows the history, though. Today, the island becomes a favorite location for tourists. Most of them come from Jakarta. They want to retreat from daily routines. Apart from its beauty, the island is located near to Java Island. Thus, visitors can reach it without hassles. Are you interested?

The Nuance

There are two options. First, it is Macan Besar Island. It is famous for a beach resort. That means you can get a comfortable accommodation, there. Another choice is Macan Kecil Island. It is an uninhabited and serene isle. Thus, it is suitable for those who want to relax. Both the islands feature clear and blue sea. There are some bushes and in the island. If you visit Macan Besar, there is a wooden pier. It is long and sturdy. Usually, visitors use it for sightseeing and fishing!

Exploring Macan Island

The best attraction in Macan Island is the resort. Many people also call it an eco-resort. It combines natural and modern designs. Do you wonder about the foods? Well, most of the menus are made of organic plants. The foods are simple but tasty. Don't forget to eat their fresh fruits, as well! If you want entertainment, there is a clubhouse. You can also watch DVDs, read books, and socialize with other guests. It gives you an opportunity to make new friends.

Next activity is snorkeling. The resort provides you snorkeling gears. The guests are allowed to rent them. Once you have obtained the equipment, it is time to visit the snorkeling spots. For those who need direction, the staff may help you to reach those locations. In the afternoon, you should go back to your room. Next thing to do is enjoying the sunset. The best spot is on the pier. The sky starts becoming red as the sun sets beautifully.

It is true you must spend some money to stay in the resort. No worries. It is a worthy expense. In fact, you get the best facilities and accommodations. Both snacks and drinks are free. There are numerous fun activities, as well. These include snorkeling, sunset sightseeing, beach walking, and island hopping. In the next day, you are able to visit nearby islands, especially Macan Kecil. It is a good place to eradicate your stresses. Don't forget to carry your camera, though. Some parts of the islands are worthy for photography.

Nearby Attractions

- Pulau Tidung
- Pulau Semak Daun
- Pulau Pari

How to Get There

It is easy to reach Macan Island. Travelers only need to visit Marina Ancol. From dock 6, you can take a speedboat to reach your destination. Make sure you depart in the morning. Usually, the boat is ready at 8 am. The trip is about 90 minutes. Your primary objective is the eco resort. Once you reach the resort, make sure to rest first. In the next day, you can do what you want to do in Macan Island.

Where to Stay

- Macan Besar Resort

Matahari Island

A Hidden Paradise in Matahari Island, Thousand Islands Regency

For those who love water sports, Matahari Island is on your list. A vacation in Thousand Islands Regency is worth tons of experience. There are many isles available, so you can explore them all. Matahari is one of them. It is also called Sun Island. What makes it so special? There are hundreds of corals in the sea near to the island. They are beautiful and colorful. Thus, it becomes a primary destination for snorkeling. Not to mention it is the home of gorgeous villas. On top of that, the environment is neat and clean!

The Nuance

The first impression of Matahari Island is its water. It represents deep, but a calm sea. During holidays, you may expect some swimmers in the sea. There are several snorkelers, as well. From afar, you can see their light life vest. They look happy and you can join them later. Once you reach the island, a gorgeous atmosphere may hit you. Near to the beach, there are shady and big trees. In the horizon, you are able to witness neighboring islands.

Exploring Matahari Island

Sun Island has similar characteristics to other islands in "Kepulauan Seribu". Though, it has a better quality in terms of cleanliness and nature. The thing is you are not allowed to fish. The government protects nautical lives there. These include corals and fishes. Due to this strict rule, tourists are able to witness flawless nautical beauty. No wonder, more people come to Matahari Island for snorkeling. It is a comfortable experience. Thanks to clear and safe water. It doesn't have to be scuba diving. You can swim in the sea freely. Make sure to only explore the shallow water, though.

Matahari Island becomes natural conservation for fishes. In the sea, you can find tame fishes. It is possible to feed them, too. Thus, you should carry some bread or crackers. It is quite tempting to feed those fishes, after all. In the evening, you can enjoy good times near to the dock. It is a good spot for enjoying dinner. The best menu is seafood. These include grilled squids, shrimps, etc. The guests can choose the food freely. The villa management takes care of everything!

Your next feasts are in Laguna snack bar and bamboo bar. Those are popular places for tourists. Not to mention there is a discotheque. It is going to be a wonderful experience. A combination of the sea atmosphere and a clubbing activity is quite outstanding. In some occasions, you may encounter foreign tourists. They come from Germany, Korea, Japan, and much more. This explains why Matahari Island is as popular as Tidung Isle.

Nearby Attractions

- Melinjo Island
- Sepa Island

How to Get There

There are two routes to Matahari Island. First, it is in Muara Angke. From here, it takes about 4 hours using a traditional motorboat. Another route is in Marina Ancol. It takes approximately 2 with a speedboat. Both of the routes are recommended. It depends on your location, after all. If you choose the second route, it is going to be a faster trip.

Where to Stay

- Matahari Island Villas

Melinjo Island

Camping in Melinjo Island, Thousand Islands Regency

In Indonesia, you can find Melinjo Trees. There is a beautiful island with the same name, though. It is part of "Kepulauan Seribu". The name is Melinjo Island. The location is near to Harapan Island. In the past, the island became a base of Indonesian Custom. Today, it is a tourist destination, especially for campers. A good landscape and solemn nature make a perfect camping site. Not to mention it is the home of wild birds and lizards. The thing is you should have a permit in visiting the island. After all, it is a private island.

The Nuance

In the beach, you may encounter soft and sloping landscape. In the back, there is a higher land. It is located under the trees. Also, it becomes campers' favorite spot. Shady trees and sea scenery make a perfect atmosphere for them. During holidays, you may find several visitors in such location. If you don't act fast, you won't get a good spot! For many, holidays aren't a good time to visit Melinjo Island. Many campers have already been there before you. As the result, you aren't able to get a good location to build a tent.

Exploring Melinjo Island

Once you have arrived at Melinjo Island, you should ask

permission from the keeper. He lives in there, after all. No worries. He is a good person. Almost all tourists are allowed to explore and stay a few days on the island. As long as you don't cause a ruckus, you are free to roam around. If you come for camping, both west and east parts of the island are a perfect choice. Those are quieter and more comfortable than other spots. Not to mention they are located near to the pier.

It is an independent activity. Campers don't depend on any tour agency. That means you must prepare everything by your own. This gives you a unique experience, though. You are going to enjoy living in nature. These include building a tent, gathering woods, and cooking. In the evening, you should ignite a bonfire. The mood becomes better if you carry a guitar and sing along with your friends. Sometimes, you can hear the sounds of nature, especially the bats. Have no fear. They cause no harms to visitors.

In the morning, you can see a stunning sunrise from the pier. Next, it is time for snorkeling. The reefs may amaze you! There are numerous types of fishes such a bat fish, eel, lionfish, and even sea turtles. In the afternoon, there is a mesmerizing sunset. You can enjoy it from the same place. Some crows are wandering around. This creates a rustic atmosphere. At night, don't forget to make a cup of coffee. Overall, it is going to be a wonderful camping experience.

Nearby Attractions

- Gosong Rangat Island
- Sepa Island
- Harapan Island

How to Get There

The way to reach Melinjo Island is similar to that of nearby islands. From Muara Angke, you should take a boat to Harapan Island. From there, you can use a local boat to your last destination.

Where to Stay

- Camping

1945 Museum

1945 Struggle for Freedom Museum

1945 Struggle for Freedom Museum is located at Menteng Raya Street 31, Central Jakarta. In 1938, a Dutch businessman named LC Schomper, built a hotel called Schomper, I at Menteng Area. The hotel was built as a place to spend nights for high officials of the Nederland, foreign Entrepreneurs, and high officials of local government.

During the colonization of the Japanese Empire in Indonesia youth and it was turned into a boarding house and Education center for Indonesian Youth in order to learn nationalism. Soekarno (1st Indonesian President), Mohammad Hatta (1st Indonesian Vice President), Adam Malik Chaerul Saleh and many other youth generations of Indonesia are involved in the educations process inside. The name of the Hotel Schomper 1 Hotel then turned into Gedung Menteng 31 Building). As time went by, the Gedung Menteng 31 was used for many purposes. It was once used as office of Ministry of Manpower arrangement, National Boards of the Generation of 1945, and Jointly Secretariat of Nation Works Organization (secretariat Bersama Golongan Karya) - Embrio the GOLKAR Party.

After the building was renovated and repaired Gedung Menteng 31 was officially established as Museum Joang 45 on August 19, 1974, by former President Soeharto and former governor of Jakarta Ali Sadikin. The name, Museum Joang 45' is chosen as the building has played great role on the Independence if Indonesia and could become a site for the inheritance process of invaluable struggle values in 1945. The Museum is open from 8.00 am to 3.00 pm on Monday to Friday

Ancient Inscription Museum

Ancient Inscription Museum
Ancient Inscription Museum is located at Tanah Abang Street 1, Central Jakarta. The piece of land of former Dutch cemetery called Kebon Jahe Kober has been arranged to be a shaded and green garden with various kinds of tropical plants grown on it, and has become a place of intensive supports for both artistic and historical values. This land was designed as cemetery for the Dutch, especially for officials and important prominent figures.

After Indonesia gained its independence, this land was still used for the public, especially by Christian people. Since 1975 Kebon Jahe cemetery was closed, and by seeing the existing potentials, preservation and rearrangement of the selected inscriptions and gravestones were performed on that land of 1,3 ha. On 7 July 1977 the DKI Jakarta Governor Ali Sadikin, inaugurated pat of the land of the former Kebon Jahe cemetery to be an Inscription Museum. Knowing the inscription would mean to know the works of talented designers, painters and sculptors cast as a materialization of deep expression of the people who gave the order or the users, because as if inscription was able to talk on what we need to know.

This Museum displays gravestones from various Dutch names and prominent figures like Major General J. H. R. Kohler, Dr. W.F. Stuterheim, Dr. F. Roll, Pieter Erberveld and others. There is a row of other names like Olivia M. Raffles, Miss Riboet, Soe Hok Gie and others who was berried or moved to this location since the 17th century until the 1900s.

Basoeki Abdullah Museum

Basoeki Abdullah Museum in Cilandak Sub-district, South Jakarta City
Jakarta Special Region has many valuable museums, and all of them are worth a visit. For those who are into arts, Basoeki Abdullah Museum is a recommended place to explore. Just like the name implies. The museum stores arts collections and paintings of Basoeki Abdullah, including shadow puppets, statues, paintings, weapons, and masks. Currently, the museum is managed by the Ministry of Education and Culture. It also opens for public, so everyone is allowed to enter it. Sometimes, tourists can also join seminars and studies. Not to mention they

have the chance to join a workshop, publishing numerous works like articles, biographies, and catalogs.

The Nuance

The size of the building is about 600 m2 and it consists of two floors. Both the nuance and environment are clean. Thanks to the great management. What about the history? Well, the construction finished in 2001 and it was inaugurated by I Gede Ardika. Before dying, Basoeki Abdullah's will was to gather and retain his collections in a house and turned it into a public attraction. With the help of the government, his house was renovated into a museum, displaying his lucrative arts collections. On top of that, tourists consider it as a recommended tourist spot in West Cilandak.

Exploring Basoeki Abdullah Museum

As mentioned before, the museum retains Basoeki's art collections and other valuable items. In fact, there is a memorial room! In terms of number, there are about 720 collections and 3,000 books or magazines. Once visitors enter the building, they may find several rooms on the first floor. These include a living room, masks and shadow puppets exhibition hall, and Basoeki's bedroom. The fact is he was mysteriously murdered in 1993 in his bedroom. No wonder, the aura of the room seems mystical and strange.

The second floor contains a gallery, where Basoeki's paintings reside. There are about 50 of them, but the locals say there are more than 100 of them. In this floor, visitors may find 3 exhibition rooms. The first one consists of scenery paintings only, while the second room consists of famous people like R.A Kartini, Ferdinand Marcos, and much more. What about another room? It displays abstract paintings. Among all the paintings, the most famous one is called "Flora dan Fauna". The rumor has it, the eyes of the boy in the painting may move accordingly to the audience's movement!

Overall, Basoeki Abdullah Museum is a hidden treasure of Jakarta tourism. It is a recommended place to witness the collections of such famous artist. In fact, some students come to the museum to do a field study. In fact, taking pictures is allowed there. What's next? Another charm is the entry fee, which is quite cheap for everyone.

Nearby Attractions

- Harry Darsono Museum
- Layang-Layang Museum

- Cilandak Town Square

How to Get There

The museum resides in Cilandak Sub-district, South Jakarta City. To be exact, it is located in Keuangan Raya Street 19. From Soekarno-Hatta Airport, the distance is 32 km and it takes about 35 minutes to reach the place. Also, the best route to use is Jakarta Outer Ring Road. That's all.

Where to Stay

- Maven Hotel
- Park 5 Hotel
- RedDoorz
- Blue Sky Hotel

Central Museum

The Batavian Society of the Arts and Sciences was established on this site in 1778, by U.M.C. Rademacher under the auspices of the Batavia Association of Arts and Sciences, it offers historical, prehistorically, archaeological and ethnographic aspects of Indonesia through its extensive collection of artifacts and relics which date as far back as to the Stone Age. It has one of the most complete collections of bronzes and ceramics dating back to the Han, Tang and Ming Dynasties. The Museum has one of the finest numismatic collections in the world, including cloth and money, which was used on several islands until recently. The religious art section is filled with statuary and sculpture salvaged from sites of Hindu, Buddhist and Islamic edifices. Its collection of cultural instruments, household utensils, arts and crafts provide an introduction to the life of the various ethnic groups, which populate Indonesia. This museum is popularly known as Gedung Gajah or "Elephant Building" because of the stone elephant offered by King Chulalongkorn of Thailand in 1871, placed on the front lawn of the building.

Due to its rapid growth, the building was transformed into a museum in 1862. As well as being excellent displays of everything Indonesian, leather puppet shows, called Wayang Kulit, are performed every second and last Saturday night of the month at the Central Museum in Jakarta.

Fantasy Land

Dunia Fantasi or 'Fantasy World' / 'Fantasy Land' is a fun and theme park designed to entertain the visitors into the fascinating worlds of modern science and technology. A recent addition to Jakarta's growing recreation facilities is the Fantasy Land, a 9.5 hectares (23.75 acres) entertainment park located inside the

Ancol Dreamland. Planned to eventually become a part of a 200-hectares (500-acres) park designed to usher the visitors into the fascinating world of modern science and technology, the present facility takes them on an imaginative tour of Old Jakarta, Africa, America, Indonesia, Europe, Asia and the Palace of Dolls. Each of the areas is designed to give the visitor a feel of the region he is visiting through features and architecture of the area at a certain period of its history and by the use of animated puppets in the Palace of Dolls.

This colossal recreational resort faces the enchanting Jakarta Bay. Its prime attraction is Fantasyland, an amusement park that keeps children, especially, entertained the entire day. Fantasy world is the host of many of the amusement rides and the most popular of them is a roller coaster ride called Halilinter. The park has other themes also. Art buffs and tourists who search of souvenirs should visit Pasar Seni art and handicraft market. Others might like to check out Sea World (a giant aquarium) for an educational tour on marine life or Ancol Water Park for yet more fun. The Ancol Marina operates as the gateway to the neighboring Thousand Islands. The facilities take visitors on imagination tours of Africa, America and Indonesia through some breath taking games. The park also offers a number of restaurants and souvenir shops.

Fine Art Museum

Fine Art and Ceramic Museum

Fine Arts and Ceramic Building Museum was built in 1870. At the beginning the building was used as Dutch Judiciary Institution or Raad Van Justitie, then when Japan colonized Indonesia and the fight for Indonesia freedom occurred the building was used as military dormitory. Furthermore it was used as West Jakarta Mayor's Office in 1967. In 1968 until 1975 it was used as office of DKI Jakarta Museum and History Official. On Agust 20 th 1976 it was announced officially as Fine Arts Gallery Building and now become Fine Arts and Ceramic Museum.

This museum has around 400 fine arts, which consist of many different techniques and materials, such as sculpture, graphic, wood totem, sketch, and painting batik. Among those collection there are some masterpieces, collections that useful for the art history in Indonesia. They are "Revolution Bride" painting by Hendra Gunawan, "Lebak Regent" painting by Raden Saleh. "Mother Give Sick" painting by Dullah, "Tritura Paramilitary Troops" painting by S. Sudjojono, and "Self-Potrait" painting by

Affandi. Traditional classical sculpture from Bali, magical and symbolic wood totem by Tjokot and families, Totem and wood sculpture by modern artists, such as G. Sidharta, Oesman Effendi. Then followed by academy graduate artists creation, like Popo Iskandar, Achmad Sadali, Srihadi S. Fajar Sidik, Kusnadi, Rusli, Nashar, Zaini, Amang Rahman, Suprapto, Irsam. Mulyadi W, Abas Alibasyah, Amri Yahya, AS Budiono, Barli, Sudjana Kerton and many other artists from various regions. There are also plenty of ceramic collections in this museum, consist of local and also foriegn ceramic. the local ceramic comes from Aceh, Medan, Palembang, Lampung, Jakarta, Bandung, Purwakarta, Yogyakarta, Malang, Bali, Lombok, etc.

This Museum has also Majapahit ceramic from the 14 th century, which show beatiful extraordinary characteristic and have history value with various shapes and functions. The foreign ceramic of various shapes, characteristics, functions, and styles from China, Japan, Vietnam, Thailand, Dutch, Germany, and Middle East. The greatest numbers are from China, especially from Ching and Ming Dinasty. Fine Art's and Ceramic Museum has specific souvenir for visitors, like post cards, fine art's book, handicraft, sketch, fan, cute sculpture, etc. The Museum is open daily from 9 am to 3 pm on Tuesday to Sunday. The Museum is closed on Monday and Public Holidays.

Indonesian Orchid Park

Indonesian Orchid Park in Pinang Ranti Rural Community, East Jakarta City

What is a recommended place to enjoy a vacation in Jakarta Special Region? Well, many options are available. For example, Indonesian Orchid Park resides in East Jakarta City. All people living in Jakarta should have heard about it. The place stores various species of orchids and becomes a great place for tourists, collectors, and traders. The park was inaugurated in 1993 by Soeharto (the 2nd President of Indonesia), and today it becomes a recommended spot for a recreation. Most of the visitors are orchid lovers, after all. However, it is also suitable for everyone, including families and travelers.

The Nuance

The location is about 1 km from TMII and it is near to At-Tin Mosque. Once tourists reach the location, they can see a wide parking area, decorated with Balinese Frangipani flowers. In fact, the parking lot can accommodate hundreds of vehicles. The thing is visitors should pay the parking fee. Next, there is a hall with the shape of Balinese gate. It also features a fiberglass roof that makes the nuance a bit tropical and hot. Another unique feature is the trash bins, having the shape of a yawning frog.

Exploring Indonesian Orchid Park

According to the history, Indonesian Orchid Park was constructed to respect women's rights. The idea came from Soeharto's wife, actually. As if, it represents the beauty of Indonesia. Not to mention it becomes a famous tourist spot in Jakarta. The park displays numerous types of orchids and all of them come in a beautiful appearance and satisfying fragrant. There is a famous one, which is called "Anggrek Bulan". In fact, it is the signature orchid of Indonesia. The government even included it in the list of National Flowers or Puspa Pesona.

Apart from tourists, visitors come to the park for studying orchids. The fact is a research center resides there. Those who work in laboratory unit keeps developing orchid seeds until reaching the age of 1.5 years old. Later, they might distribute them to kiosks for sale. As for tourists, the park becomes both a marketplace and sightseeing. It is highly recommended to come with more cash, as they would spend it on beautiful orchids and seeds, after all. As for reference, Bromelia is considered the best seller there. Have no worries. The price is definitely affordable.

Once visitors explore all parts of the park, it is time to visit a renowned restaurant called Karimata. The location is near to Indonesian Orchid Park, after all. It is the place to enjoy delicious foods like grilled fish and spicy sauces! That dish indeed represents Indonesian's culinary, which is spicy and flavorsome. Overall, the restaurant becomes the right option to end the adventure in the park. That means tourists would go home in full stomach!

Nearby Attractions

- Ragunan Orchip Park
- Ragunan Zoo
- Jakarta Catherdal
- TMII

How to Get There

For those living outside Jakarta, it is better to head to Soekarno-Hatta Airport first. From there, tourists can directly head to Pinang Ranti Rural Community, East Jakarta City. The park is located in TMII Raya Street, after all. It takes about 1 hour and 20 minutes from the airport and the distance is 44.7 km.

Where to Stay

- Fiducia Pondok Gede Hotel

Indonesian Stamp Museum

Indonesian Stamp Museum in Cipayung Sub-district, East Jakarta City

Before the existence of smartphones and other advanced gadgets, people are into philately. They collected different types of stamps that came from distinct nations. In this case, a tourist spot like Indonesian Stamp Museum would be a great vacation destination. The location is within TMII Complex, situated in East Jakarta. So, what is inside the museum? It is a no brainer. The building displays many collections of stamps and other valuable items. With such attractions, the museum becomes a top-notch tourist spot in Jakarta Special Region, especially for those who love philately.

The Nuance

In terms of appearance, Indonesian Stamp Museum applies the combination of Balinese and Javanese architecture. The gate has the shape of a temple and there is a pendopo, which is located in the midst of the yard. In front of it, there is a globe with a small dove statue on it. It represents the delivery of mail all over the globe! The next feature is the statue of Hanuman (the Monkey King). The reason is Hanuman was Rama's messenger in reaching Shinta, who was abducted by Rahwana. Near to the statue, there is an old mailbox, which was owned by the Dutch back then.

Exploring Indonesian Stamp Museum

Now, it is time to explore or get around the museum. Before enjoying numerous stamp collections, tourists should learn a bit history of Indonesian Mailing. A tourist guide would provide the information to visitors, after all. The fact is people used palm leaves to send messages to others. They might cook those leaves first prior to writing messages on them. In the museum, the guests can see a sample of the leaves and the tree. Another important feature of the museum is the presence of a giant stamp, displaying the face of Tien Soeharto (the wife of the 2nd president of Indonesia). It is quite majestic.

Many exhibition halls are available, displaying post equipment, diorama, and some old stamps from different eras. These include Daendels Raffles and VOC stamps. Near to the location, tourists can see miniatures of VOC ships, post trains, post horses, etc. On the wall, there is the picture of Rowland Hill, who was the

World's Father of Stamp. He was the one who invented the stamp system as the sign of acquaintance in sending mail.

What's more? The next famous attraction is the replica of Penny Black, which is the first published stamp. It is said such stamp was released in 1840 by Batavia Post Office. Such legendary stamp has King Willem III's picture on it. In the block II, tourists can learn the production of stamps. What's in the block III, actually? It is the famous Indonesian stamp, which was published during the war of Independence. It is also worth an observation.

Nearby Attractions

- Keong Mas Park
- Freshwater World
- Indonesian Museum
- Sacred Pancasila Monument

How to Get There

For outsiders, the first destination is Soekarno-Hatta Airport. Once tourists get there, they can take any local transportation service to Cipayung Sub-district, which resides in East Jakarta City. To be exact, Indonesian Stamp Museum is located in TMII Street. It is easy to find, after all.

Where to Stay

- Santika Hotel
- Asri Hotel
- Gerbera Hotel

Jakarta History Museum

Located in the historic Old Jakarta Kota area, Taman Fatahillah square offers three of the city's most interesting museums. Once the heart of the colonial administration in the 18th century the square underwent a major restoration in the 1970's. A fountain in the middle of square once as the main water supply for the former colonial capital. The Portuguese cannon on the north side of the square is reportedly an impressive font of fertility. Jakarta History Museum is the one displaying the history of the development of the City of Jakarta, both the events and the community, from the prehistory until these present days. This museum is located in a building of cultural property which in the past known as Stadhuis, the City Hall of Batavia. As written on an inscription of the Museum collection, the building was constructed in 1707 by the city government of Batavia during the period of VOC and Governor General Abraham van Riebeeck inaugurated it in 1710. This building is located in front of a park, which in the past was known as Stadhuisplein, the City Hall Park, and now it is called Taman Fatahillah.

Since 1970, the surroundings of Taman Fatahillah have been declared as Cultural Property and it was totally preserved. This effort was the beginning of the development of the historical area of the City of Jakarta, carried out by the Government of DKI Jakarta. The Museum of History of Jakarta was inaugurated on 30 March 1974 for being the center for collection, conservation and research for all kinds of objects of cultural property related to the history of the City of Jakarta and at the same time becomes a center for education, study and recreation for the community. Due the very long course of the history of Jakarta, the collection of this Museum are highly varied in shape and consist of objects being the heritage of the prehistorical period until the beginning of the 20th century.

There are another replicas of the Tugu Inscription from the age of Great King Purnawarman, forming evidence that the center of the Kingdom of Tarumanegara was located in around the seaport of Tanjung Priok. Further, a map of the 16th century and the replica of the Padrao monument of the Portuguese represent the historical evidence of the age of Sunda Kelapa Harbor. The period of Jayakarta is the beginning of the establishment of the City bronze cannon and through various drawings and maps of the 17th century. Furniture collection of Betawi style from the 17th, 18th and 19th century is the richest collection and belongs to the most complete one in the world. This collection is very interesting since the association reflects of the community of Batavia City with various cultural elements from Europe, especially Dutch, China, India and Indonesia.

Jakarta Museum of Kites

Jakarta Museum of Kites in Cilandak Sub-District, South Jakarta City
Visiting Jakarta Special Region is worth the expense, as many types of attractions are available. One of them is located in Cilandak Sub-district, which is called Museum of Kites. The locals call it Layang-Layang Museum, actually. As the name suggests, the building displays various types of kites, coming in different colors and shapes. It opens every day, but holidays. Not to mention the entry fee is quite cheap. Mostly, the visitors are students, kids, and families. They want to witness unique collections of kites that come from different regions, after all.

The Nuance

In terms of size, Jakarta Museum of Kites is not quite big. That means it would be a bit uncomfortable during weekends, as many visitors would come, especially the kids. However, the place offers a homey nuance with shady trees and beautiful plants. In fact, there are some benches and a gazebo, on which tourists can relax. The design of the museum is quite traditional but majestic! This features facilities like toilets and a mushola, which are both clean and neat. When it is about foods and drinks, the guests can buy these near to the entry point (ticket counter).

Exploring Jakarta Museum of Kites

So, what can people do there? In a nutshell, the guests are allowed to get around the museum, exploring all available rooms. Though, it is better to enjoy a documentary video regarding kites and related information, which is provided near to the entry point. Once it is done, they may perform a small tour, witnessing many collections of local and foreign kites. These are well-kept in the primary building, which has the shape of Joglo House. Have no worries. All those kites come with a thorough description. Still, hiring a tour guide is quite recommended.

According to the information, it was Indonesian, who flew the first kites instead of Chinese. Is it true? Well, the most significant proof is the pre-historic paintings, displayed on the wall of Sugi Patani Cave in Muna, Southeast Sulawesi. In the past, local people use Kolope leaves and pineapple fibers to fly kites. That means such fun activity has been done since about 4,000 years ago. On the other hand, the Chinese flew their first kites since 2,000 years ago. This fact would be quite satisfying for visitors, for sure.

Jakarta Museum of Kites exhibits three different categories of kites, including cultural, competition, and sports kites. When it is about the biggest one, there is one with the size of 3 meters. All of those kites indeed attract photographers. The problem is it requires a proposal prior to taking pictures inside the museum. As visitors, everyone should obey such kind of policy, after all. As an alternative, they can learn how to make a kite or other items like ceramics. Kids can also learn how to paint and make Batik.

Nearby Attractions

- Basoeki Abdullah Museum
- Harry Darsono Museum
- Ragunan Zoo

- Pondok Indah Mall

How to Get There

The museum resides in Kamang Street 38, Pondok Labu Sub-district. Actually, it belongs to South Jakarta City. If travelers come from Soetta Airport, they may spend about 40 minutes to reach the location. The distance is 33.5 km, after all. As for the tip, they should take Jakarta Outer Ring Road, which is the fastest route.

Where to Stay

- Maven Hotel
- Zahabi Hotel
- Mirdhas Place
- Park 5 Hotel

Jakarta Old Town

Kota Tua in Jakarta Special Region - Jakarta Old Town
Jakarta is the capital of a beautiful country called Indonesia and it has become a center of government for decades. Aside from being a business and governance center, it also has a splendid history and culture. For example, there is one called Kota Tua or Old Old Town. As the name suggests, it holds numerous historic structures, which were used during the colonialism era. The fact

is Jakarta (Batavia) was once considered a strategic spot to trade during the 16th century. Today, the site becomes tourists' favorite destination to hang out and feel the old atmosphere of the city.

The Nuance

Kota Tua Jakarta or the Old Town of Jakarta is located in Kunir Street 23 A, Tamansari. It belongs to West Jakarta City, actually. Despite the small size, which is about 1.3 km2, it has lots of attractions including historical buildings and several spots to hang out. Most of the structures are old museums, but an old harbor also resides near to the area. Tourists usually come there during the afternoon or at night when the nuance feels more comfortable. Some people are also seen in the morning as they enjoy fresh air and do some sports like jogging.

Exploring Jakarta Old Town

Due to its historic atmosphere, Jakarta Old Town is suitable for walking around and jogging. That means visitors can take advantage of the nuance to find peace and eradicate stresses. They can explore the area and see numerous old buildings land museums. Some parts of it are used by local vendors to promote their items, as well. These include foods, accessories, etc. For those who want to visit the museums, they must come before 3 pm (the closing hour). The thing is they should avoid coming at noon when the temperature is hot. Thus, the best time to visit is in the morning.

The main charm of Old Town is the formation of old museums, which are scattered near to each other. These include Bank Mandiri, Bank Indonesia, Arts & Ceramics, and Wayang Museum. Each of them offers distinct beauty so tourists should visit them all. As mentioned before, visitors should come before the closing hour. For those who look for a simpler activity, they can enjoy riding a bike around the area. Have no worries. Some locals provide bikes for rent to tourists and the price is quite affordable.

Another unique attraction in Jakarta Old Town is the presence of local artists, those who dress like a statue, soldiers, Dutch lady, and much more. They move around the area and often become an object for photography. Visitors are even allowed to take pictures with them, in fact. At the end of the adventure, tourists should enjoy local snacks called Kerak Telor. It is both crispy and tasty!

Nearby Attractions

- ITC Mangga Dua
- Mangga Dua Morning Market

How to Get There

The best transportation service to use to reach Kota Tua Jakarta (Jakarta Old Town) is the commuter line. The fact is that the area is accessible from any location, so it is quite reachable. For those who don't want to feel any hassle, riding a taxi is the simplest way to head to the site despite the expensive fee.

Where to Stay

- Ibis Mangga Dua Hotel
- RedDoorz Hotel

Jaya Ancol Dreamland

Jaya Ancol Dreamland (Taman Impian Jaya Ancol)
Taman Impian Jaya Ancol, an amusement park in north Jakarta, Indonesia, is one of the most attractive places serving the densely populated city of Jakarta. It has all the adventures people crave for; Sea World, Fantasy World, Atlantis Water Adventure and Marina Beach. This is Jakarta's largest and most popular recreation park. It is built on reclaimed beach land at the Bay of Jakarta, having, sea and freshwater aquariums, swimming pools, an artificial lagoon for fishing, boating, bowling, an

assortment of nightclubs, restaurants, a steam-bath and massage parlors. The Ancol complex includes a Marina, Dunia Fantasi (Fantasy Land), a golf course, hotels and a drive-in theater. The "Pasar Seni" or art market has a varied collection of Indonesian handicraft, paintings and souvenirs on sale. At a nearby open-air theater art performances are held using the local dialect.

Inside the Ancol Dreamland, there is Ancol Art Market, it is outdoor art market likely recreational place where we will be most tempted to purchase something. Items include antiques, handicrafts, painting, potters, and knickknacks. With many of the artisans working on site, it is a paradise for souvenir hunters and art lovers. This colorful open-air market located in the Ancol Amusement Park provides the unique experience of not only buying quality Indonesian arts and craft, but also a chance to see and meet the artisans at work. We can watch puppet makers, wood-carvers, painters, and many other craft makers from throughout the archipelago cheerfully working on their creations. At this art and handicraft market, visitors get to watch Indonesian artists creating their masterpieces. Hundreds of artists from all over the country congregate here to exhibit their work, making the spot a fascinating place for tourists and art connoisseurs. We can even get a portrait of our self-done. Both traditional and modern art and crafts are on display, including paintings, sculptures, traditional Indonesian wayang kulit (leather puppets), gemstone jewelry and many other artistic products. Art performances are frequently held at the Art Market (Pasar Seni) inside the Jaya Ancol Dreamland on Jakarta's beach. They normally range from wayang kulit shadow plays to folk dances and modern drama. This location is open Monday to Saturday, from 2 p.m. to 9 p.m.; Sunday, from 10 a.m. to 9 p.m.

Keong Mas Park

Keong Mas Park in Cipayung Sub-district, East Jakarta City
Lots of tourists have recognized TMII, which is located in Jakarta Special Region. Such famous park consists of several attractions and one of them is called Keong Mas Park. The location is near to Air Tawar Museum and it offers numerous rides for kids. Even though it costs some money to enter the park, it would be worth the expense. Usually, the park would be quite crowded on weekends and holidays. Most of the visitors are families with kids, after all. They come to try all the water rides and enjoy beautiful landscapes of the park.

The Nuance

Once tourists enter Keong Mas Park, they may notice a unique robot. The shape of the head is similar to a tree, and it is able to talk a bit. The thing is the voice is quite strange and creepy. This explains why some kids get startled when the robot talks. Near to it, there are some rides like a mini roller coaster, mini carousel, etc. That spot is the heaven for kids and families, for sure. What's more? In the right part of the park, visitors can find a mini version of Jurassic Park! Some dinosaur robots reside in such location.

Exploring Keong Mas Park

Here is the fact. Keong Mas Park is TMII's new attraction. The size is about 7 hectares and it was inaugurated in 2015. It offers many types of rides like Nirwata Kisar, Dinosaur Adventure, Pirate Ship, and much more. There is even a theater and education corner. The management named it "Teater Legenda", actually. It presents a cartoon that tells the legend of Panji Asmoro and Dewi Sekartaji. Usually, visitors would come to the theater after trying all the rides. It is because the room of the theater is quite refreshing.

The next popular attraction is the Dinosaur Adventure Park. In that site, tourists are able to interact with robotic dinosaurs. These can even make noises and spray water. Some of the famous dinosaur species are T-rex and triceratops. Still, many others are also seen on that site, so visitors should not miss those statues. That means photography is also recommended there. Not to mention some unique structures reside in the park, including a Pendopo. It becomes an extra charm in the park and elevates visitors' moods.

Apart from those attractions, Keong Mas Park offers a clean environment. No wonder, visitors would feel comfortable there. Next, there is a café called Barong, offering some snacks and drinks. It is situated at the corner of the pond. This way, tourists can ride a duck boat and buy snacks directly in such café. Another nearby facility is a souvenir store that comes with affordable items. However, it is located outside the park.

Nearby Attractions

- Insects Museum
- Sacred Pancasila Monument
- Indonesian Stamp Museum
- Freshwater World

How to Get There

Keong Mas Park is part of TMII, after all. In order to reach the location, tourists should head to East Jakarta City. To be exact, the location is in TMII Raya Street, Cipayung Sub-district. It would take 41 minutes from Soekarno-Hatta Airport and the distance is 43 km. As for the best route, it is Jakarta Outer Ring Road.

Where to Stay

- Santika Hotel
- Asri Hotel
- Gerbera Hotel

Marina Jaya Ancol

This is the port to reach Pulau Seribu (Thousand Islands) in the Bay of Jakarta, as well as the center for marine sports ad recreation. This is a special port for yachts, motor and sailboats, and the scattered islands in the Bay of Jakarta. This is also the place for marine recreation and sports where each facility is amply provided; water cycles, canoes, sail boats, fishing gear and many others. Stalls along the beach serve drinks and snacks while tents are available for sunbathers and sea lovers.

Ancol Marina is the most usual departure point, speed boats leaving regularly to whisk us away from the city heat to the cool, palm fringed beaches of paradise. However chartering a boat is also possible for anyone with a more adventurous spirit. Jet skies canoes, sail boats wind surfing and waterskiing are all to be found, along with all kinds of fishing gear we may need for hire. Numerous stalls along the beach serve drinks and snacks while tents are available for sunbathers and sea-lovers.

Pelangi Island, a small island that located about 70 kilometers from Marina Ancol or about one and a half hours by speedboat, is a near Sepa Island and Pantara Island. The similarities of these beautiful islands are that they have sandy beaches and sit in the middle of a clean blue ocean. Pelangi Island had thronged by Italian and Japanese tourists. Presently, thanks to the domestic tourists and expatriates, the island economy is sustained.

Martha Tiahahu Park

Martha Tiahahu Park in Kebayoran Baru Sub-district, South Jakarta City

Those who live in Jakarta Special Region should have heard about Martha Tiahahu Park. That beautiful park is located in Kebayoran Baru Sub-district and it belongs to South Jakarta City. The fact is the park resides near to famous bus station called Blok M and Pertamina Hospital. The government constructed it in order to fulfill the needs of green open spaces in Jakarta. It also becomes a significant vacation destination for tourists. People keep coming to the park to do some fun activities like sightseeing and relaxation. Plus, they may gather either with friends and families.

The Nuance

The size of the park is 20,960 m2, and it is considered one of the biggest parks in Jakarta. No wonder, lots of people often gather there either in the morning or afternoon. Decorated with green grasses, a monument, fountain, and big pool, the park offers a comfortable nuance. The other features are roosters and dove cages. That means visitors can freely witness both animals and plants there. Not to mention there is a sign of the park that comes with white and green color. Thus, visitors can notify it easily.

Exploring Martha Tiahahu Park

The best attraction in the park is the formation of flowers, plants, and trees. They are quite comforting and shady. Next, visitors can simply witness cute birds and roosters. The thing is those animals are well-kept in cages, which means they won't cause any troubles. In terms of facilities, the park provides benches, trash bins, and toilets. With all those benefits, it is likely visitors would spend much time in the park. They can do many things like enjoying fresh air, resting, playing with their kids, and photography. Martha Tiahahu Park is also suitable to eradicate stresses.

Apart from recreation, the park is also famous for its history. Here is the question. Why is the name? Martha Christina Tiahahu is recognized as a female hero in Ambon. She fought bravely against the Dutch during Pattimura War in 1817. Due to her bravery, the government decided to use her name for the park. It also has a good management, so the environment is quite clean and comfortable. Also, it has a good concept and beautiful landscape. Even the trash bins have unique shapes like dinosaurs, deer, elephants, etc.

With the presence of many trash bins, the park teaches visitors not to litter carelessly. In fact, visitors are not allowed to smoke and step on the grasses. This way, people can learn the importance of nature. Also, they have the chance to eradicate stresses at once, as Martha Tiahahu Park is suitable for those who live in a big city. It is the simplest solution to deal with boredom and tensions. The combination of clean environment, fresh air, and lush trees is indeed rejuvenating.

Nearby Attractions

- Ayodya Park
- Mayestic Market
- Gandaria City Mall
- Polri Museum

How to Get There

Martha Tiahahu Park is located in Kebayoran Baru Sub-district, South Jakarta City. To be exact, it resides in Sisingamanganraja Street. For those coming from Soekarno-Hatta Airport, it takes 35-40 minutes to reach the park and the distance is 29.8 km. As for the best route, it is Jakarta Inner Ring Road.

Where to Stay

- Falatehan Hotel
- Kebayoran Hotel
- Melawai Hotel

Maritime Museum

Maritime Museum is located at Pasar Ikan, 1 North Jakarta. Initially these building served as warehouse for storing spices. The Dutch East Hindia Company started the constructions in 1652 and expanded in the years later. In 1976 the premises were handed over to the municipal government of Jakarta and preparation were started to convert them into a museum. The maritime museum was officially opened on July 7th, 1997. The objective of this museum is to converse, maintain, protect and expose the Indonesia maritime and fishery tradition. A variety of traditional Indonesia boats with their very specific shapes, equipment and decorative trimmings reflect a high-standard maritime heritage. Apart from these props, there also miniatures of modern ships on display. Navigational tools, anchor, the model of light house, antique canons and many more items form part of the museum's collection.

Indonesia is an archipelago country with a territorial extent of 5,1 million square kilometers. Out of that extent, 3,1 million sq. Km or 60 % are waters. This geographical condition, of course, contains various kinds maritime culture. It may be true when later there has been a poem contained in the song of the Indonesian children saying Our Ancestors W ere Seamen. The Maritime Museum is the only one in Indonesia presenting maritime specific theme. The building used for it was the former warehouse for storing spices which in the past known as Westzijdsche Pakhuizen. The construction was done in three stages; it was commenced in 1652 until 1774.During the Japanese occupation (World War II) these warehouses were still used for storing Japanese owned goods for war purposes. This

Museum, inaugurated by the Governor of DKI Jakarta, Ali Sadikin, in 1977, has now around 1670 collections from various maritime aspects, displayed in the forms of natural and cultural heritages.

Those Collections are, for example, traditional boats (originals and models) found in the Nusantara archipelago like Bugis boat, Phinisi (Bugis cargo boat), Pandekawang, miniature of Alut Pasa boat from Kalimantan and Warship from Maluku called Kora-Kora. Sea biota, sea archaeology, fisherman equipments, fishery anthropology and folklore, history of shipping relations between Nusantara and the Netherlands, Maritime tourism, information on the Navy, paintings of maritime prominent figures and other important maritime information. In the context of its development, the Maritime Museum often holds collaboration with the related Foreign Embassies and Governmental Agencies.

National Monument

The National Monument, or "Monas" as it is popularly called, is one of the monuments built during the Sukarno era of fierce nationalism. The top of the National Monument (Monas) is Freedom Square. It stands for the people's determination to achieve freedom and the crowning of their efforts in the Proclamation of Independence in August 1945. The 137-meter tall marble obelisk is topped with a flame coated with 35 kg of gold. The base houses a historical museum and a hall for meditations. The monument is open to the public and upon request the lift can carry visitors to the top, which offers a bird's eye view on the city and the sea.

Go early to beat the crowds and the haze. It is easy for the less physically able as lifts take visitors to the top. The diorama exhibition in the basement gives such a distorted view of Indonesian history - thanks to the dictator Suharto wanting to brainwash the nation - it's amusing. This imposing obelisk is Jakarta's most famous landmark. Construction started in 1961 under President Soekarno but was not completed until 1975, under President Soeharto. The monument houses a couple of museums. The Freedom Hall depicts Indonesia's struggle for independence through a series of dioramas, whereas the Hall of Contemplation displays the original Declaration of Independence document and a recording of the speech. An elevator takes one to the observation platform, which commands a bird's-eye view of the cityscape.

National Museum

The Museum is situated on Merdeka Barat Street. Currently the National Museum houses collections of 109,342 objects under the categories of prehistory, archaeology, ethnography, numismatics-heraldic, geography and historical relics. In 1994, the museum started with is expansion project. The new building, constructed in the same architectural style as the old, comprises an arena for theatrical performances and more spaces for exhibitions. The museum curators provide detailed information and guidance on collections-related subjects during working hours. The daily activities at the National Museum include collecting, caring for and protecting collections and providing information on the museum and its collections to visitors and the public at large. The Indonesian Heritage Society (HIS) voluntarily assists the museum in handling the inventory of the collections.

The museum's Conservation and Restoration Division is dedicated to conserving and restoring the collected objects in order to protect them from possible damages and loss. The staffs also take preventive measures against possible damages or loss through manual, alarm and control system. This Museum is open from 8.30 am to 2.30 pm on Tuesday, Wednesday, Thursday and Sunday, from 8.30 am to 11.30 am on Friday, and from 8.30 am to 1.30 pm on Saturday. The Museum is closed on Monday and Public Holidays.

This museum is also has supporting with such tourism facilities. A small gift shop located in the entrance hall has the same opening hours as the rest of The Museum. It offers a selection of books, postcards and reproductions of various exhibits. The front courtyard can accommodate cars and tour buses. Visitors are kindly asked to refrain from smoking, eating and drinking in all areas of the Museum, and are prohibited from touching the exhibits.

Pancasila Sacred Monument

Pancasila Sacred Monument Cipayung Sub-district, East Jakarta City
One of the reasons in visiting Jakarta Special Region is its history. It is because the capital of Indonesia holds numerous historical places, on which tourists can explore. One of them is located in Cipayung Sub-district Pancasila Sacred Monument. It was built as the recommendation of Soeharto, the second president of Indonesia. The purpose was to recall the struggle of Revolution Heroes in retaining Pancasila (the ideology of the nation). At that time, Indonesia was under the threat of communism. Those

heroes include Suprapto, Haryono, Siswondo Parman, DI Panjaitan, Sutoyo Siswomiharjo, and A.H. Nasution.

The Nuance

Being a recommended tourist spot, the monument becomes popular over time. It is also because the landmark is situated near to a famous "Lubang Buaya". Once tourists reach the monument, they can learn a bit history of those revolution heroes and their clothes! The color of the monument is predominantly white and it has Garuda Pancasila statue on its wall. Not to mention the statues of the heroes reside on the foundation. The fact is the monument is surrounded by lush trees, so the nuance is comfortable and shady.

Exploring Pancasila Sacred Monument

Some tourists are attracted in the history of the monument, so they come to the site to learn about its history. In this case, the help of a tourist guide or the locals is quite helpful. Despite the fee, it would be valuable information. Apart from its history, the landmark becomes a favorite object for photography. Visitors can simply take some pictures of it or take selca. One thing, they are not allowed to get too close to it. It is also important to take care of the environment. That means littering is extremely prohibited.

Actually, some unique attractions are located near to the monument. First, it is the Deadly Well (Lubang Buaya). It was the pit where revolution heroes were killed. Next, there is the House of Torment. As the name suggests, it was the place where the heroes were tortured before getting killed by the communists. In the past, it also became a local school. With these facts, the aura of the house seems creepy and dark. Though, it is a worthy location for tourists. In that site, the management presents a diorama regarding the rebellion of Communist Party and the struggle of local heroes.

The next attraction is the Command Post. It was actually the base of Lieutenant Colonel Untung, the leader of PKI (Communist Party) when he was planning for the abduction of revolution heroes. Today, it becomes a significant tourist lure near to Sacred Pancasila Monument and it displays historical items like petromax, glass cabinet, and sewing machine. These items became the part of the history, after all. No wonder, they are considered valuable and worth keeping.

Nearby Attractions

- Indonesian Stamp Museum
- TMII
- Transportation Museum
- Freshwater World

How to Get There

Sacred Pancasila Monument is located in Pondok Gede Raya Street, Cipayung Sub-district. It belongs to East Jakarta, actually. For those coming from Soekarno-Hatta Airport, the trip takes about 1 hour and 20 minutes. The distance between those locations is 50.2 km, after all. For the fastest route, they can either take Jakarta Inner Ring Road or Pantura Street.

Where to Stay

- Cipayung Asri Hotel
- Budeh Agung Hotel
- Asri Hotel

Ragunan Zoo

A Perfect Vacation in Ragunan Zoo, South Jakarta City
Situated in South Jakarta City and it is recognized as the first zoo in Indonesia. In the past, it was situated in Cikini, but the government decided to move it to Ragunan in 1964. The inauguration was in 1966 and it has become a recommended

vacation destination for both local and foreign tourists. Apart from the fame, the zoo stores majestic and beautiful animals. Not to mention it has an easy access, so any travelers can drop by without hassles.

The Nuance

In terms of size, Ragunan Zoo has the width of about 140 hectares. As mentioned before, it stores numerous species of animals and their habitat. At least, there are 295 species of animals, which are kept well. There is also an iconic statue of an elephant, which often becomes an object of photography. Near to it, a serene pond resides with lots of natural ornaments like plants and small trees. With such shady and comfortable atmosphere, the guests would be happy to explore it. On top of that, the environment is quite clean.

Exploring Ragunan Zoo

Like other zoos, Ragunan offers many types of animals, including mammals, reptiles, primates, fowls, and many others. The thing is the number of animals has decreased, as compared to the past. Still, the rest of them are quite eye-catching! This explains why many visitors carry a camera to take some pictures of the animals. When it is about the most favorite area, it is definitely the Schmutzer Primate Center. In fact, it becomes the biggest primate preservation on the planet and it keeps various primates like gorillas, chimpanzees, white apes, gibbons, etc.

What's next? Some animal attractions or shows are conducted regularly, including the snake dance and an elephant riding. Those are usually performed on weekends and tourists should pay some money to enjoy them. As an alternative, tourists can enjoy screenings regarding animals or other topics. Thanks to the management. Visitors would get lots of fun and entertainment there. Plus, good environment maintenance makes the zoo more comfortable to explore. Despite such excellent upkeep, tourists should never litter or cause harm to either the zoo or animals! That's the prime rule to obey when visiting Ragunan Zoo.

The next activity is to explore all parts of the zoo. Both the scenery and nuance are quite satisfying! Moreover, the zoo provides some interesting services like a mini train and bicycles, which are rentable. That means tourists can get around the zoo without spending too much energy. Moreover, the rent fee is affordable.

Nearby Attractions

➢ Ragunan Lake

- TMII
- Cilandak Town Square
- Jakarta Museum of Kites

How to Get There

Ragunan Zoo is located in Pasar Minggu Sub-district, South Jakarta City. To be exact, it resides in Harsono Street 1. For those coming from Soekarno-Hatta Airport, it takes about 36 minutes as the distance is 35.8 km. The best route to take is Jakarta outer ring road, actually.

Where to Stay

- Sahati Hotel
- RedDoorz
- Kyriad Suites

Sea World

Inside the Ancol Dreamland complex, Sea World is a high tech modern huge aquarium exhibiting the special and diverse tropical marine life found throughout the Indonesian waters. Stroll through Freshwater World and Micro world, see beautiful tropical fish and corral reefs, and get friendly with marine life at the Touch pool. A theater screens movies about the underwater world and a necessity is the Antasena Tunnel, a walk-through acrylic tube that gives first hand experience of life under the sea. This giant aquarium proudly introduces visitors to more than 4,000 fish and sharks from 300 species. Sea World has great many attractions to its credit; it has a Dolphin Show that is quite popular and a gallery, which showcases many of sea creatures from all over the world. Some times people find it better in comparison to Sentosa Island, one of the most popular destinations in Singapore.

Come and enjoy the deep-sea panorama while strolling through an 80-meter tunnel. The fascinating creatures live in some 500 million liters of seawater and are fed three times a day (some hand-fed). The attraction also features a theater, which plays three educational films in English and Bahasa Indonesia. Open Monday to Saturday, from 2 p.m. to 9 p.m.; Sunday, from 10 a.m. to 9 p.m.

Shadow Puppets Museum

This artistic building stay at Pintu Besar Utara Street 27, West Jakarta, was built in 1912, previously as land of a church, which was built in 1640 under the name of De Oude Hollandsche Kerk (The Old Dutch Church). In 1732 it was renovated and its name was changed into De Nieuwe Hollandsche Kerk (The New Dutch

Church). The church building was once totally destroyed by an earthquake. Bataviasche Genootschap van Kunsten en Wetenschappen (Batavia Society of Arts and Sciences), that was an institution dealing with science and Indonesian culture bought this building.

The institution then delivered this building to the Stichting Oud Batavia (Old Batavia Foundation) and on 22 December 1939. It was made a museum under the name of Oude Bataviasche Museum (Old Batavia Museum). In 1957 this building was delivered to Lembaga Kebudayaan Indonesia (Institute of Indonesian Culture) and on 17 September 1962 it was delivered to the Ministry of Education and Culture of the Republic of Indonesia, which later was delivered to the DKI Jakarta Administration on 23 June 1968 to be made Shadow Puppet Museum, which inauguration was carried out on 13 August 1975.

Shadow Puppet (commonly known as wayang) in Indonesia, especially on Java Island, was originally a product of the Royal Court culture. It was first used as an instrument of worship to the ancestors, and after the Hindu culture entered Indonesia iaround the 5th century, it developed shifting of values. The world of Indonesian shadow puppet got characteristically influence especially in term of story, like the Ramayana (the Story of Rama) and Mahabharata (the Great Bharata), making the form of presentation keep on changing and with wider range in performance and in the theme of the story. In its later development the Indonesian shadow puppet had become such tradition, that it has been capable to hold out in the supporting community consisting of various elements. Visitors of this Museum are invited to know various characters, attitude and behavior of the story from various regions through the performance of shadow puppet that has weight of high value in our culture and viewing a number of collections of shadow puppet like wayang kulit, wayang golek, patung wayang, topeng wayang, wayang beber, wayang kaca, gamelan (traditional music instrument set) as well as wayang paintings.

This Museum also displays various collections of wayang and dolls from friendly countries like Malaysia, Thailand, Suriname, China, Vietnam, France, India and Cambodia. It is not merely to be an object for recreation, study for students/ devotee can be carried out in this Museum, and this Museum even can be used as venue for training, documentation center and research on shadow puppet, and it can be used as inter-regional and international media on cultural knowledge. To support its existence, in this Museum wayang staging and attraction of wayang making are periodically organized.

Situ Babakan

Betawi Culture Settlement in Situ Babakan, South Jakarta City

One of the best charms in Jakarta Special Region is its culture. As for reference, there is Situ Babakan, which is located in Jagakarsa Sub-district. It is the place to witness and learn some traditional cultures of Betawi. The locals manage it well, as the effort in retaining valuable Betawi Culture. Actually, Babakan is an artificial lake that resides in a local settlement. Tourists recognize it as either a recreational site or culture tourism. They also come to the location for fishing and sightseeing. Regardless of the reasons in visiting Situ Babakan, the place is worth an exploration!

The Nuance

When it comes to the nuance, Betawi Culture Settlement looks simple and traditional. It is true most of the visitors are interested in the local life and its culture. However, some of them are also interested in spending a vacation in the lake. The atmosphere is peaceful and the villagers are friendly. Even foreign tourists can approach them without hassles. There are also several village gates or entry points, displaying the name of the location. Thus, tourists won't get troubled to find it. On top of that, the condition is neat and clean!

Exploring Situ Babakan

The fact is the government has chosen Situ Babakan as the place to retain Betawi Culture. No wonder, visitors are able to enjoy various attractions and local foods there. First, they can observe the local's life such as trading and farming. Some villagers may also show the guests regarding how to make Betawi's signature snacks. Not to mention tourists have the chance to make new friends. The fact is the villagers also consist of newcomers, coming from Center Java, Kalimantan, and others. There are about 3,000 households there!

The best time to visit Situ Babakan is during the birthday of Jakarta Special Region, as many types of attractions are conducted at that time. These include drama shows, musical performances, dances, and much more. As an alternative, visitors can come anytime for a recreation. The reason is the village retains its serenity and shady atmosphere. The lush trees and a beautiful lake are definitely charming. That means such settlement is also suitable for a family outing and relaxing. The air is fresh and the weather is nice. Furthermore, the clean environment even makes it better.

Another lure in Situ Babakan is the culinary. Many signature foods of Betawi are available there, including Kerak Telor, Ketoprak, Laksa, Soto Betawi, Apem Cake, and much more! As for the beverage, there is famous Pletok Beer! Even though those foods and drinks are affordable, tourists should carry more money. It is likely they are going to try them all, so excess expenses are unavoidable. Also, they need the money to rent a boat later. They won't miss the chance to explore the lake, after all.

Nearby Attractions

- Spathodea Park
- Bambon Fishing Site
- Miring Park
- Tabebuya Park

How to Get There

As mentioned before, Situ Babakan is located in Jagakarsa Sub-district and it belongs to South Jakarta City. For those coming from Soekarno-Hatta Airport, the distance would be 42.2 km.

That means they need to spend about 55 minutes to reach the location. Also, the best route to take is Jakarta Outer Ring Road.

Where to Stay

- House of Eva
- RedDoorz
- Amare's Pavillion

Sunda Kelapa

Sunda Kelapa, better known as Pasar Ikan (meaning fish market) is located at the mouth of the Ciliwung River. The fish catch of the day was auctioned in the early morning at the old fish market. The street leading to it was lined with shops selling all sorts of shells, dehydrated turtles, lobsters and mostly everything the seafarer might need. This 500-year-old harbor area was a vital link to markets of the outside world for the 15th century kingdom of Pajajaran. It was formerly the harbor town of Sunda Kelapa where the Portuguese traded with the Hindu Kingdom of Pajajaran in the early 16th century. Since than this port has belonged to the portuguese and Dutch.

Dutch domination of Jakarta and the rest of Indonesia began from this area, whereas the remnants of Kasteel Batavia, an old fort and trading post of the Dutch East Indies Company can still be seen now. Sunda Kelapa is at present a fisherman's wharf and an inter island port. Tall-misted Bugis schooners from South Sulawesi anchoring there offer a picturesque scene. They belong to one of the last-fleets of sailboats in the world and still ply the seas between the islands, as they did centuries ago, carrying merchandise.

Tough little remains of bustling old Sunda Kelapa except the name, the harbor is still one of the most important calls for sailing vessels from all over Indonesia. The magnificent and brightly painted Makassar schooner called Pinisi is still an important means of transporting goods to and from the outer islands. This is one of the finest sights in Jakarta.

Wander around the old Sunda Kelapa port, watching gangs of sinew-stretched coolies smoking pungent clove-laced cigarettes unload cargos of timber, coal and spices from stunning wooden schooners. Hire a dugout canoe and paddlers and enjoy the waterside scenery. The boats also go to the nearby old fish market, which can be reached easily by foot from the port and is free to enter. Work starts here at 3am and it's essential to arrive by 6am to see the best of the action.

T.I.M Art Center

T.I.M (Taman Ismail Marzuki) Art Center

Jakarta is overflowing with hip clubs and bars catering to all tastes. But if we want a snapshot of Jakarta's current artistic pulse head to Taman Ismail Marzuki in Cikini. The center of Arts in Jakarta, Taman Ismail Marzuki, also known as TIM, is a complex located on Cikini Raya Street 37, Jakarta. Those who are looking for traditional and contemporary arts might find this place useful. This complex acquired its name from the great Indonesian musician, Ismail Marzuki, whose statue guards the entrance gate. It hosts the Institut Kesenian Jakarta (Jakarta Institute for the Arts) and Jakarta Platenarium. The arts institute is the only one of its kind in Indonesia and the first local college entirely dedicated to the training of performing and visual arts. There are modern, state-of-the-art theatres and cinemas, more traditional auditoriums, street performers and a cornucopia of restaurants and bars offering basic but tasty food and drink from all over Indonesia. The patrons range from the young, trendy, keen-to-be-seen set to bohemian artistes debating the latest trends.

The focal point of cultural activities in Jakarta is the Jakarta Art Center, known as Taman Ismail Marzuki or TIM in short. It is said to be the largest of its kind in Southeast Asia and consists of exhibition halls, theaters, an academy of arts, an archives building and a planetarium. A monthly programmed of events, available at hotel counters, includes exhibitions, plays, musical and poetry recitals, dance performances, folk art and drama from the various regions of Indonesia. Facilities include an indoor and outdoor theater, exhibition halls, two art galleries and a cineplex.

TMII

Beautiful Indonesia in Miniature Park (TMII)
Taman Mini Indonesia Indah (Beautiful Indonesia in Miniature Park) is Indonesia's answer to every visitor's prayer to see the magnificent archipelago in just one day. An extensive park to get a glimpse of the diverseness of the Indonesian archipelago, it represents Indonesia's 27 provinces and their outstanding characteristics, reflected most strikingly in the exact regional architecture of the province. An extensive theme park set in over 100 hectares on the outskirts of Jakarta; the All Indonesian islands are realistically reproduced in miniature in a central lake and around the lakes, there are pavilions. Each pavilions is representative of each province firm the traditional architectural

style in miniature to a wonderful display of cultural items and exhibits. The park's centerpiece is a beautiful artificial lake. The complex was the brainchild of Madam Tien Soeharto, the late Indonesian first lady.

It also has its own orchid garden in which hundreds of Indonesian orchid varieties are grown. There is also a bird park with a walk-in aviary, a fauna museum and recreational grounds with a swimming pool and restaurants. The special interest here at Taman Mini is the Museum Indonesia. A richly decorated building in Balinese architecture, it houses contemporary arts, crafts and traditional costumes from the different regions of the country.

Cultural performances, events, and even local delicacies from the provinces are prepared regularly, especially during weekends and holidays, to showcase Indonesia's rich cultural heritage. The park is open seven days a week, giving guests ample time to explore and enjoy the sights. And if a day tour is not enough, visitors can spend the night at the 'Desa Wisata' or 'Wisata Remaja' serviced accommodations.

Transportation Museum

Transportation Museum in Cipayung Sub-district, East Jakarta City

Jakarta Special Region has lots of recommended tourist spots to explore. For those visiting Cipayung Sub-district, they should drop by in Indonesian Transportation Museum. The government constructed the building in retaining, collecting, researching, and displaying the history and development of national transportation. Today, it is well-managed by the Ministry of Transportation and becomes an interesting vacation destination for tourists. According to history, the construction began in 1984 and it was conducted by the wife of the 2nd president of Indonesia. When it is about the inauguration, it was in 1991.

The Nuance

The gates and fences of the museum are predominantly blue. It also features several modules and buildings, one which the guests can explore. On the top of the main gate, there is a symbol of Ministry of Transportation. No wonder, it was under the supervision of such department. Inside the museum, visitors can view numerous types of historical transportations and their importance to the nation. Moreover, the government provides it as the center of education and recreation for tourists. Not to mention the environment is clean and neat, so it would be quite comfortable for visitors.

Exploring Transportation Museum

The fact is the exhibitions are done both inside and outside the museum. There are several halls, which are called modules. These include the main, land, air, and sea module. Also, the management displays many forms of vehicles, including diorama, photos, miniatures, and the real ones. When it comes to the guests' favorite attraction, it is definitely Indonesian traditional vehicles. For examples, there are Andong, Cikar, Perahu Layar, Bendi, and Becak. All of them are unique and valuable. They also become wonderful objects for photography, so carrying a camera is a must.

In the land module, visitors can see numerous types of land transportations, including traditional and modern ones. In fact, there is Cikar Damri, which was the first armada of DAMRI and had a significant role during the indepencence of Indonesia. At that time, it was used as a military logistic vehicle both in Mojokerto and Surabaya City. Aside from it, there is also an old locomotive, bicycles, etc. The land module is only the beginning, as tourists have other places to explore like air and sea modules.

In the sea module, visitors can learn the presence and service of marine transportation. These include passenger ships, floating decks, containers, and much more. What about the air module? Well, it displays planes, airport equipment, etc. All of them are also worth an observation. Next, it is time to visit static exhibitions, which are located outside the museum. It shows historical locomotives and buses. Also, an old lighthouse resides in that area. It is more than 100 years old, in fact.

Nearby Attractions

- Indonesian Stamp Museum
- Keong Mas Park
- Sacred Pancasila Monument
- TMII

How to Get There

Here is the fact. The museum is located in TMII Raya Street, East Jakarta City. Travelers only need to take either a bus or taxi to Cipayung Sub-district. For outsiders, it is better to head to Soekarno-Hatta Airport first. Later, they might continue the trip to the museum.

Where to Stay

- Desa Wisata Hotel

- Asri Hotel
- Santika Hotel

Souvenir Center

SMESCO Indonesia Jakarta Souvenir Center and Its Miscellaneous Indonesian Products

The beautiful country of Indonesia is a holiday paradise because of its wonderful traditional culture, culinary, and stunning scenery. As on any occasion when visiting a country, people tend to purchase local souvenirs and gifts for those loved ones back home with whom they would like to share their experiences. In Jakarta, the capital city of Indonesia Country, tradition culture and craft were born and cultivated. During your visit to this capital city, why not taking time to explore something unique to Jakarta Souvenir Center, either by yourself, or with family or good friends? The ideal place to find these priceless items of Jakarta Souvenir Center can be found at the SMESCO Indonesia Company. SMESCO itself stands from Small & Medium Enterprises and Cooperatives, where one of its purposes is to promote and market the local products made by the small & medium enterprises to domestic and international market.

At the SMESCO, there are selected not only traditional craft-work goods, but goods which are also unique and interesting from all provinces of Indonesia area. SMESCO has SME Tower and SMESCO Building that are designed by each Indonesia provinces and display a range of SMEs superior products of the provinces. With Provinces Pavilion that located on floors 15, 12, 11 and 3 in SMESCO Building, you will impress the diversity of Indonesia. SMESCO takes pride in presenting selection handicraft to customers from Indonesia and abroad alike. For the Small & Medium Enterprises sector, SME Tower is a new emblem in achieving the development and marketing local products. And as a business center in Jakarta, SME Tower provides modern and complete facilities with a big expectation. This building has expected to become 'one stop shop' building for local and international customers who want and need to buy the Indonesia local products. The center boasts a diverse and unique assortment of arts and crafts outlets retailing a quality selection of clothing, home adornments, toys, and other such gifts tapping into the tastes of each shopper.

SMESCO Indonesia also cooperates with a number of partners of other countries. It aimed to have a good opportunities for Indonesia's products access and market. With sustained supports, highly creative and innovative SMEs will contribute significantly to create employment and ensuring sustainable growth. SMESCO encouraged the local SME companies to display their product there, so the visitors able to buy directly the products from all Indonesia provinces without come to each provinces. The process in submitting the product to be curated and displayed in SMESCO is easy, just bring the product, then the product will be curated, and if the product passed the curation process; the product will eventually be displayed. You can find many things at SMESCO Indonesia, from the handicrafts, traditional clothing; including many batik collections, shoes, bags; and of course the food. So, let's visit SMESCO Indonesia at Jl. Gatot Subroto Jakarta, and collect souvenir original from all provinces in Indonesia.

Restaurants

Casa Cisca	**Giuseppecorica Pastries**
Plaza Semanggi, Third Floor 3A / 12B	Sampit V Street 2
Phone: (021) 25536332	Phone: (021) 7237418
Chianti Classico Bistro	**Domus**
Mega Kuningan Street	Veteran I Street 30, Central Jakarta

Phone: (021) 5761601

LA Porchetta
HR. Rasuna Said Street Kav. 62
Phone: (021) 5210601

Sinbad
Raya KS. Tubun Street 2, West Jakarta
Phone: (021) 5308366

The Duck King
Asia Afrika Street, Central Jakarta
Phone: (021) 57932032

Sim Yan
Kalibesar Barat Street 46
Phone: (021) 69041188

Samudra
BRI Tower II (Center Park 8th Floor)
Jend. Sudirman Street Kav. 44-46, Central Jakarta
Phone: (021) 5713600

Back 2 Beef
Hang Lekir Street 15, Kebayoran Baru
Phone: (021) 7396275

Club Fez
Kemang Raya Street 788
Phone: (021) 7192677

Phone: (021) 3447288

Al Nafoura
Le Meridien Hote;
Jend. Sudirman Street Kav. 18-20, Central Jakarta
Phone: (021) 2513131

Anatolia
Kemang Raya Street 11A, South Jakarta
Phone: (021) 7194617

Golden Ming
The Acasia Hotel
Kramat Raya Street 73-81, Central Jakarta
Phone: (021) 3903030

Golden Palace Restaurant
Summer Palace Restaurant
Menteng Raya Street 29, Central Jakarta
Phone: (021) 3142989

Kuah
"Bakwan & Noodle House"
Radio Dalam Raya Street 1A, South Jakarta
Phone: (021) 70723362

Celebes Setiabudi One
HR Rasuna Said Street Kav.62
Phone: (021) 5211949

Selera Vegetarian
Boulevard Raya Street, RA-19/12 Kelapa Gading, North Jakarta

	Phone: (021) 45843139
Padmanadi Pakin Street 1 A/11-A12, North Jakarta Phone: (021) 6625132	**Maitri** Keamanan Raya Street 29A, West Jakarta Phone: (021) 6398396
Mudita Batu Ceper Raya Street 7, Central Jakarta Phone: (021) 3806739	**Marunda** Santika Hotel AIPDA KS. Tubun Street 7, West Jakarta Phone: (021) 5361777
Galeria TC Kemang Raya Street 24A, South Jakarta Phone: (021) 7194270	**Planet Hollywood** Gatot Subroto Street, Kav. 16,
South Jakarta Phone: (021) 5267827	**Tony Roma's** Panin Bank Center, Jend. Sudirman Street Phone: (021) 7202735
Front Row Jend. Gatot Subroto Street, Central Jakarta Phone: (021) 5747231	**Chilli** Mh. Thamrin Street 11, Central Jakarta Phone: (021) 3146537
Dinning Room Brawijaya Raya Street 26, Central Jakarta Phone: (021) 7258668	**Ayam Bakar Taliwang** Panglima Polim IV Street 125, Kebayoran Baru, South Jakarta Phone: (021) 7252863
Ratu Kuring Buncit Raya Street 135, South Jakarta Phone: (021) 7996886	**Satay Senayan** Tanah Abang 2 Street 76, Central Jakarta Phone: (021) 3847270

Travel Agents

Carmeta Ampuh Tour & Travel Service
Outer Ring Road Kamal Raya Street, D8/10 West Jakarta
Phone: (021) 54350533

El John Tours & Travel
Wisma Indovision 12th floor
Raya Panjang Street Z/3
Phone: (021) 5824888

Cita Tour
Sunter Hijau Street
Raya Block S4/12 Sunter Hijau, North Jakarta
Phone: (021) 65303354

Matahari Tour & Travel
Jend. Sudirman Street Kav. 28
Phone: (021) 5212212

PT. Dream Tour & Travel
Pejagalan 1 Street 1 BE, West Jakarta
Phone: (021) 6918525

Air Antariksa Travel
Bintaro Utama IX Street HA1/21, Bintaro Jaya, South Jakarta
Phone: (021) 74864843

Mega Wisata Jakarta
Medan Merdeka Timur Street 17
Phone: (021) 3511555

Talenta Tour & Travel
Sunter Paradise 2 - K29
Phone: (021) 65831507

Sahabat Travel
Maleo Raya Street
Block JC 4-02 Bintaro Jaya
Phone: (021) 7451718

Good Day Tour
Boulevard Artha Gading Street I/27, Kelapa Gading North Jakarta
Phone: (021) 45856763

Kurnia Djaja Wisata Tour & Travel
Bintaro Utama I Street E/08-09, Bintaro Jaya, South Jakarta
Phone: (021) 73888183

Jakarta Weekend Guide

How to Spend a Weekend in Indonesia's Vibrant, Diverse Capital?

A direct flight between London and Jakarta on Garuda Indonesia has made south-east Asia's most culturally-diverse capital accessible from the UK as never before. Some 10 million people live here, but almost all have roots elsewhere, resulting in an exuberant blend of Javanese, Balinese, Chinese, European and numerous other cultures. Jakarta is the capital of the world's most populous Muslim-majority nation, but Hinduism, Christianity, and Confucianism also thrive. Tolerance rules, exemplified by lively restaurants serving spicy meals washed down with cold beer, and an on-the-pulse clubbing scene that pounds until the wee hours.

Gridlocked traffic is a frustration, but seeking out pockets of history and culture amid the maelstrom is part of Jakarta's allure. Sunda Kelapa docks and the old town of Batavia are reminders of Dutch colonial times, while the hip hotels and glass skyscrapers of Menteng spin you back to the 21st century.

Day one
Take a view

The high-speed lift which whizzes up 56-storey Jakarta Skye Tower (1) (ismaya.com/skye) in 10 dizzying seconds feels like a fairground ride. On a clear day (or night) the views are dazzling. There is an open-air terrace and restaurant, but you can go for coffee or a cocktail depending on the time of day.

Take a hike
During three centuries of colonial rule, Batavia on the southern fringe of Jakarta Bay, also now known variously as Kota or 'Old Jakarta', was the commercial hub of Dutch Indonesia. Get a taste of this era with its trappings of imperial power by starting in the Taman Fatahillah square (2) flanked by stately structures such as the Jakarta History Musuem (3) in the old Stag Huis (town hall), built by the Dutch in 1710.

Follow the Kasar Besar Canal (4) bordered by crumbling European-style mansions, up to the photogenic 16th-century wooden Kota Intan drawbridge (5). Continue down the canal to the Bahari Maritime Museum (6) in an old Dutch East India Company warehouse.

Then climb the Syahbandar Watchtower for commanding views over the port.

Lunch on the run

The northern edge of Kota district spills into a warren of cobbled alleys where burning incense wafts from Taoist temples and markets buzz with busy food stalls. This is "Glodok", traditionally the enclave of the Chinese community and the place to graze a bewildering array of street treats. You'll find crispy roast duck wings on wooden skewers and steamed dumplings stuffed with ground beef or water chestnuts, all wrapped in banana leaf. More exotically, Jalan Pancoran street (7) specialises in Rujak Shanghai Encim, a concoction of cuttlefish, spinach and peanuts drenched in tangy red sambal sauce. Or if your craving is for pig's intestines stewed in a sweetish pulp, sekpa is the stuff to sniff out.

Window shopping
Strung along a canal in the leafy Menteng district, open-air Jalan Surabaya market (8) is a teeming amalgam of stalls and shops bringing together Dutch, Javanese, Balinese and Chinese artefacts, both antique and modern. You will find fragments of Jakarta's diverse history are on display: barnacle-encrusted Delft porcelain salvaged from wrecked galleons; Javanese puppets; Chinese jade dragons; carved wooden statues from Borneo; and traditional masks from the Indonesian archipelago's tribal fringes. Good haggling skills essential.

An aperitif
Sip a cold Bintang beer at the Batavia Marina Bar (9) (bataviamarina.com) on the seafront next to old Sunda Kelapa port where rows of resplendent pinisi-masted schooners are moored. Watch stevedores load cargo bound for the so-called "Thousand Islands" of Jakarta Bay, in dock scenes reminiscent of past centuries.

Dine with the locals
Mix with pop stars, actors, politicians and other glitterati at the whimsical Dapur Babah (10) restaurant (tuguhotels.com) just off Merdeka Square. Owner Anhar Setjadibrata and his daughter Lucienne might be there to welcome you to the pair of old merchant houses they have restored and stuffed with mementoes from the city's history. Especially striking is the collection of Hindu, Buddhist and Chinese statues. The term "Babah" refers to the time when Dutch-influenced Javanese women married Chinese settlers. This fusion of cultures resulted in a style of cuisine exemplified by dishes such as tahoe goreng petis fried tofu with sweet shrimp paste.

Day two
Out to brunch

Savour a rich brew of Java coffee with pastries or traditional Indonesian nasi goreng (fried rice) at Waris 13B café (11) on Taman Amir Hamzah in the fashionable Menteng district. The street is lined with terracotta-tiled houses including one where a young Barack Obama lived with his mother and stepfather after they moved to Jakarta in 1967. Round the corner is his old school, Sekolah Dasar Negeri Menteng (12); outside, a cute statue of "Barry" (as he was known) stands atop a plinth where an inscription quotes the President's proclamation: "The future belongs to those who believe in the power of their dreams."

A walk in the park
Part paved, part grassy expanse, Merdeka Square (13) is the city centre. It covers more than a square kilometre and is claimed as the world's largest city square. At its heart is the soaring National Monument (14), a 132m obelisk topped with a golden-leaf "flame", raised to celebrate Indonesia's independence from The Netherlands in 1949. Chances are there will be some sort of activity going on as you stroll through. A military parade, perhaps, or a demonstration. If not, you might find nets strung up on the grass for games of volleyball or badminton.

Take a ride

Hop on a commuter train to Gambir Station (15), the city's main railway hub on the east side of Merdeka Square, to reach Jakarta's two wonders of sacred architecture. Istiqlal Mosque (16) is made of gleaming Javanese marble and is the largest place of worship in south-east Asia with a capacity of 120,000. The triple-spired neo-Gothic Jakarta Catholic Cathedral (17) faces the mosque across a canal, a couple of minutes' walk away. The proximity of the pair is a source of pride to many Indonesians, presented as symbols of peaceful religious and cultural co-existence.

Cultural afternoon
The National Museum (18) on the west side of Merdeka Square soars to cultural heights on a par with the National Monument's physical stature. Beyond having an unparalleled collection of treasures devoted to the history, ethnology and geology of the Indonesian archipelago, this is a museum which celebrates the country's cultural diversity. Over four floors discover the origins, as well as the present manifestations, of civilisation on islands as diverse as Java, Sumatra, Bali, Flores, Sulawesi, Borneo and Papua.

Accommodation

Where to stay in Jakarta
Central Jakarta

Jakarta's main backpacker accommodation is traditionally around the Jalan Jaksa area, and plenty of basic guesthouses and homestays still exist in the area, but many haven't upgraded (or cleaned the bathroom) for decades and the whole area can feel icky and grimy. However, the-times-they-are-a-changing and a smattering of modern backpacker hostels are popping up in or close to Jakarta's tourist sights. Budget chain hotels have dominated most of the flashpacker to midrange market, while if you want to ease yourself in gently and splurge a little, some terrific mid-to high-end boutique style digs are on offer.

We have concentrated our listing on Central Jakarta (with just a couple of outliers in Kota Tua in the north), as this area is close to sights, restaurants, transport and other tourist needs, but if you are after a slightly leafier area, look around Kemang in the South or for shopping and action, Block M is another popular locale.

Kosenda Hotel

Kosenda's contemporary designed interior is no less intriguing, loaded with comfortable character-filled spaces that are both inviting and edgy. The stylish design elements include the works of contemporary Indonesian artists and reference local culture apparently the facade is based on the ornamentation of traditional Betawi houses (Jakarta's ethnic group) and this aesthetic continues into the hotel rooms.

The eight-storey hotel offers 58 compact chic rooms in three flavours, a terrific street-level restaurant serving up Peranakan delights 24/7 and a stylish rooftop bar all that is noticeably missing is a swimming pool. Room choices are tiny, cosy or a smidgen bigger, yes they are not terribly spacious, but thoughtfully designed in a way to maximise the space and feel comfortable, you just probably won't be wanting to be swinging a cat or doing a downward dog (but there is a fitness centre for the latter).

The tiled air-con rooms feature modern teak built-ins and beautiful textiles that use traditional Indonesian materials and techniques with modern flair. Pops of mustard yellow complement the neutral palette of black, white and grey with wood accents. Beds are comfortable with quality linens and furnishings include bedside tables, open storage space and a good-sized desk. We love the caddy of stationery that contains scissors, staplers and paperclips as well as the usual pens and paper so handy! Mod-cons include iPod docking stations, flat-screen cable TV, safe and tea-making facilities as standard and all but the entry level rooms add a minibar. Shuttered windows help minimise light and street noise although most offer little to no view

Compact ensuite bathrooms are stylish and functional with hot-water rainfall showers, we are just not so fond of the glass walls looking directly into the room, nevertheless it does add a sense of space and offers sufficient privacy if you are sharing. The washbasin is placed inside the main room, which some people may find a little odd too. Delightfully fragrant lotions and potions are the hotel's own blend and traditional batik robes and slippers add a nice local touch.

A carefully curated buffet breakfast that includes local specialities and gourmet coffee is included in the rate, served in the stylish Waha Restaurant, worth a visit even if you are not a guest. The Awan rooftop bar doesn't open until late afternoon, but is the perfect spot of a sundowner and if it weren't for the Jakarta skyline in the background, with the foliage and flickering candles you could almost believe you were in Bali. Another delightful spot for non-guests too, although the drinks are priced to keep you sober.

Charming staff couldn't be more helpful and Kosenda Hotel's thoughtful touches such as guidebooks to borrow and hand sanitiser by the door add to the appeal. If you are looking for comfort and style in the heart of Jakarta, Kosenda is a top pick, but if you really need to swing that cat, consider Morrissey Hotel or Artotel, both stylish and a tad roomier.

Where is Kosenda Hotel
Kosenda Hotel

127 Jalan KH Wahid Hasyim, Jakarta

T: (0213) 193 6868 F: (0213) 193 6767

info@kosendahotel.com

Coordinates (for GPS): 106º49'17.88" E, 6º11'12.79" S

Room rates: 400,000 to 1,000,000 Rp

Artotel

The hotel scores well on the coordinates too, smack in central Jakarta behind Sarinha Mall, walking distance to bars, restaurants and transport. You won't miss the street-art style facade by local artist Darbotz, nor the helix-like staircase visible through the glass frontage which opens to a spacious modern art-filled lobby. ROCO (Restaurant of Contemporary Art) open 24/7 sits to the side, embellished with the crazy critters of Swiss–based Indonesian artist Eddie Hara's murals and artworks. A gallery space on the mezzanine level displays regular changing exhibitions, and the rooms themselves come in three sizes, all featuring the work of one of five contemporary Indonesian artists each gets a floor to go wild.

The names "Studio 20", "Studio 25", and "Studio 40" refer to the size of the space and although they are mostly not huge, they are comfortable and well designed. The simple styling with raw cement walls and floors and minimalist contemporary built-ins maximises the impact of the room-sized artworks. Air-con rooms are clean and smart with comfy beds, and decent lighting. Standard amenities include a flatscreen TV, safe, iPod dock and (not-so environmentally friendly) pod coffee maker, and higher categories add a mini fridge, sofa and Studio 40 does a whole extra living room. Windows are on the small size, but it's about the art, not the view here. Compact tiled ensuite bathrooms are simple but stylish with a semi-glassed hot-water shower and modern facilities.

Artotel's rooftop bar is called BART, now we bet you think that's bar plus art? Well, ok, perhaps, but it's "Bar At The Rooftop" (we think the art is better than the names), but despite what they call it, it's a smashing spot for a sundowner, a pre-dinner cocktail or to party on all night with views across the crazy capital. Reports mention that noise from the bar can be heard on the upper floors, so if you'd prefer to sleep than party, request a lower floor. Rock up for your buffet breakfast (included in some deals) at ROCA for some recovery.

Artotel's accommodating and friendly staff are but another of the hotel's assets. We like this arty joint, but think it's a tad pricey considering there's no swimming pool (although there are bicycles if you're willing to brave Jakarta's traffic!), so shop around for deals and if it's out of your budget, go and check out the art (and the bar) anyway. If you are keen on a swimming pool, consider Morrissey as an alliterative, or you might prefer the stylish Kosenda Hotel, also sans pool.

Where is Artotel
Artotel

3 Jalan Sunda, Menteng, Jakarta

T: (0816) 1610 555 (0213) 1925 888

happening.thamrin@artotelindonesia.com

Coordinates (for GPS): 106º49'29.56" E, 6º11'18.63" S
Room rates: 400,000 to 1,000,000 Rp

Hotel Borobudur

The hotel has a place in Indonesian history along with Monas, the National Monument, and Istiqlal Mosque (which are all within walking distance of Hotel Borobudur) as they were all projects conceived in the 1960s by Sukarno, the first president of Indonesia, yet were not completed until Suharto was in power. The three share the same architect, Friedrich Silaban (to a point), although Hotel Borobudur was begun in 1963 by Silaban who designed the ground floor, but political events disrupted plans and it it was later completed by other architects.

Hotel Borobudur was intended to be the second international-standard hotel in the new republic (after Hotel Indonesia) and was designed to accommodate guests of honour of the nearby Presidential Palace, and when it opened it was the largest hotel in Indonesia. The International Style design has aged well, and the classic elegant interiors are comfortable and well maintained. Hotel Borobudur boasts six restaurants and bars (including a cigar salon) as well as eight tennis courts, a luxurious spa and if you want to beat Jakarta's traffic in style, they have a helipad too.

The most impressive feature of the hotel however is the several hectares of beautiful landscaped tropical gardens a wonderful escape from the chaos of the city streets, complete with a miniature replica of Borobudur temple and a massive swimming pool that you would have had all to yourself the day we dropped by.

Well appointed spacious rooms feature plush carpets, classically styled furnishings, all mod-cons and marble bathrooms with deep tubs. The style is refined but not stuffy, (although same may say dated) and any comforts you may require are at your fingertips. Some rooms offer fabulous city views, staff advised to book a high floor and request a good view the charming staff are obviously well trained, but this place is busy and you may have to put up with demanding other guests.

Today with so much competition, you can often find rates well under 1,000,000 rupiah, which is an excellent deal for a hotel of this standard, but also consider the club rooms which allow access to the club lounge with afternoon tea, cocktails and other extras, and if you drink alcohol, this can be excellent value in this land of high taxes on drinks.

Although staff will think you are mad, it's an easy walk to Istiqlal Mosque, Monas and several historic churches. For a more modern take on classic style, The Hermitage offers luxury (for a price) in a recently constructed hotel incorporation a heritage building. Or if your pockets are not so deep, Cordella Norwood is a decent classily styled midrange hotel with a fabulous rooftop cafe.

Konko Hostel

The paint had not yet dried when we popped in in early March 2018, but we were so impressed by the artfully designed fun spaces and the friendly owner that we reckon it's a winner. A short 300 metre walk to Jalan Jaksa backpacker area or 700 metres to Gambir Station, Konko bags an ideal location for exploring the city and although this narrow multi-storey building sits among a row of shops, the bright yellow branding is certainly eye-catching and soundproofing keeps the traffic noise at bay.

From when you first step in, everything about Konko Hostel yells cute, clever and well considered (even the business card will give you a smile). The ground floor is occupied by their street-food inspired cafe, Nonky, where you can also grab a coffee or relax with a beer (Open Mo–Su: 07:00–22:00). Take off your shoes, pop them in the fun yellow shoe holders and head upstairs to reception ("but don't take a better pair when you leave" reads the cheeky signage).

Dorms and private rooms are housed over three levels with a cosy hang-out space up top. Nooks and hallways offer seating and we spotted a kitchenette there too. Playful murals brighten the halls and depict characters you may meet on the streets of Jakarta. On offer is just about every combo you can think of from 4-bed to 6-bed and 12-bed mixed or female pod-style dorms, some with double pods, and some with ensuite or outside bathrooms as well as private single, twin and doubles with ensuite or shared facilities. Prices are room only, but breakfast can be added for 45,000 rupiah. All rooms offer air-con, keycard access and showers are hot.

Staff were a little reluctant for us to take too many photos in the yet unfinished hostel, but we hope they don't go the way of several other hostels in Jakarta and prevent potential walk in guests from having a quick look before they decide to stay, a policy we think is stupid and detrimental (what have they got to hide?).

We were only able to view the dorms and though a bit of a squeeze, they are bright and comfortable. Sturdy purpose-built pod bunks are configured both lengthways and widthwise and sport quality spring mattresses (still wrapped in plastic when we visited), individual lighting and international power sockets. Ventilation holes allow airflow and roller blinds add privacy with built-in lockers that seemed big enough for all but the largest backpack.

Although we didn't view them, private rooms add TVs, desks and seating. Share bathrooms are spacious and stylish with ample towel racks and bench space (and of course spotless, as they were new). The hang-out space enjoys a small balcony with views of the city, or just flop down in a beanbag and watch a movie on the TV, pick up a book from the library or strum a tune on the guitar.

Konko Hostel offer airport pick ups and can point you in the direction of all the fun stuff happening in the city. Although one of the pricier hostels in Jakarta, we think it's an affordable luxury, but if the budget is tight, you may consider Wonderloft or if you'd prefer more privacy, OYO 101 Apple Platinum Hotel.

Where is Konko Hostel
Konko Hostel

9J Jalan Kebon Sirih Raya, Jakarta

T: (0213) 911 127

askus@konko-hostel.com

Coordinates (for GPS): 106°49'56.51" E, 6°10'58.69" S

Room rates: Under 150,000 Rp

Morrissey

The modern glass-fronted hotel is located on the corner of busy Jalan Wahid Hasyim and Jalan Jaksa, close to bars, restaurants and sights with popular Italian restaurant, Ocha and Balla resident on the ground floor. Several styles of room are on offer and as well as the hotel's own separate restaurant, a rooftop swimming pool and gym all add up to a decent choice for your Jakarta stay.

The modern industrial style sticks to a palette of black, white and grey with dark stained wood or tiled flooring, white-painted exposed brick walls and raw cement ceilings. High ceilings and large windows add to the sense of space, while some rooms offer views, others provide no outlook with defused glass windowpanes. Studio rooms are long and narrow and other options include loft-style rooms with a living area below and sleeping above, as well as one- and two-bedroom suites.

Beds and linen are of a good quality, while comfy couches in front of flatscreen TVs and work desks are standard throughout. Larger rooms include dining facilities, with a kitchen equipped with stove top, microwave, kettle, toaster and fridge plus crockery and utensils, and there's always room service too. A quirky stylised dog sculpture adds a bit of fun to each room. Bathrooms continue the hip industrial style with white subway tiles and glass-screened hot-water showers, in some cases the bathrooms are somewhat compact and the washbasin is placed in the main room while larger rooms add bath tubs.

The swimming pool, gym and an outdoor chill-out spot bag a good view of the Jakarta skyline on non-smoggy day from their rooftop location. The narrow rectangular pool is long enough for a lap, but watch you don't hit your head on the metal poles stuck at the sides supporting the skylighted roof.

Morrissey's amenities also include a free self service laundry room (as well as a service if you desire) and as they say on their website: sorting socks is a great way to meet people! The buffet breakfast included in the rate mixes local and Western options, served in the ground-floor cafe.

Charming staff are super friendly, relaxed and not stuffy just like the hotel. If a stay at Morrissey Hotel is not within your means, but the swimming pool entices, at the time of research (March 2018) they were offering a weekend brunch and pool deal for 220,000++ rupiah (which included towels and unlimited poolside soft drinks too). Even if you don't need a kitchen, Morrissey's spacious digs and central locale are reason enough to stay.

Alternatively if a pool and size are not priorities, Kosenda Hotel and Artotel both offer style and comfort

OYO 101 Apple Platinum Hotel

A little out of place in the "hood", this thin modern multi-storey building towers above its neighbours. The hotel had only been opened a few months when we stayed in early March 2018 and had not yet come under the OYO 101 branding although the room style was much in the vein of budget chain hotel.

Simple, clean and bright tiled air-con rooms offer compact single, and more spacious twin and double options with extra comfy beds, small flatscreen TV (local channels) and hot-water ensuite. Most rooms harbour windows, but many are positioned at a high level with no outlook, however they do allow natural light to flood the rooms, shaded by blackout roman blinds for a good night of sleep. If you'd like a view, request a room at the front where the windows seem to be lower. Built-in pale coloured fake wood laminate furnishings include a small desk (although most rooms don't provide a chair to sit at it we had to borrow one from the restaurant below), hanging space, and somewhere to rest your book by (or behind) the bed. A painted geometric pastel coloured feature wall brightens without offence and moves the room up a notch from bland to welcoming.

Thick mattresses sport clean, white and cosy linen although the white towels were already starting to look a bit grey. Power points and switches are adequate and where you'd expect, operated by a keycard system. Ensuites are clean and modern, but don't offer much bench space, which can be excused a little as the shower is hot and powerful.

A hot and cold water dispenser is available on the ground floor for a hot drink or to refill your water bottle (BYO supplies) and an attached cafe makes great juices, decent coffee and standard noodle and rice dishes at very local prices and though it is a separate business, can offer room service.

Staff are friendly, but some are a little vague and we were surprised that the room was not serviced unless requested, however that wasn't mentioned at check in. When it was cleaned, little things like toilet paper were not refilled, but staff were quick to respond to our requests.

Apple Platinum Hotel is a tad difficult to find in the first instance within a labyrinth of one-way narrow lanes, but Green Apple Residence across the lane is well signposted, so look for the directions for that hotel. We found the neighbourhood safe to walk around at night, but to some folk it may seem a little intimidating and would be wise to get a taxi back.

Walk in rates quoted were higher than online which offered deals for the single room cheaper than most dorms in town excellent value. We only hope they keep it maintained. If you'd prefer more of a backpacker vibe with your budget stay, check out Konko Hostel on Jalan Kebun Sirih Raya or Wonderloft at Kota.

Dreamtel

The 80's–style facade of the eight-storey building with glass lift shafts may look dated compared to some in the street, but the rooms are smart and comfortable. Dreamtel offers Standard and Deluxe twins and doubles, triples and Suites, and unless you really want extra space, the Standard rooms are a good size and offer much the same facilities as the Deluxe (and we prefer the styling in the Standards too).

Air-con rooms are bright with wall-sized picture windows, the higher floors with city views. Black out drapes will block the light, but not the call to prayer from the neighbouring mosque. Decor is smart and inoffensive with tones of grey and white, and Standard rooms are outfitted in two styles with either polished cement feature walls and black marble patterned tiles which we think have the edge over the rooms with wood laminate features and carpeted floors (some with cigarette burns). That said, it is all a matter of taste as other than that the rooms are similar with comfortable beds, white striped sateen linen, and a room long built-in that houses a desk, luggage storage, mini fridge and tea-making bits and bobs. Other facilities include a flatscreen cable TV, safe and hanging space. Rooms are clean, but minor chips and scuffs show its age.

Ensuite bathrooms follow a similar simple modern style with glass-screened hot-water showers and ample bench space. The corners could do with a good scrub, but they are generally of a decent standard of cleanliness. Smoking rooms are available on the first and fourth floor, so non-smokers should request other floors (and vice versa).

Breakfast is included in the rate, served buffet style with many Indonesian options (better than their Western offerings). The restaurant also offers 24-hour room service, although alcohol is not on the menu (beer is available next door). Staff are bend-over-backwards friendly, but not all have a good command of English.

Dreamtel is handy to the Gondangdia commuter train station (400 metres), and Gambir for intercity trains (1.3 kilometres) and is an easy walk to Monas and the National Museum. As with many hotels in Jakarta, Dreamtel offers discounted rates on weekends making this hotel great weekend value.

Nearby alternatives with a similar rate include Grand Cemara Hotel with classic styling and a small rooftop swimming pool or the older style Cipta Hotel and tucked away in the backstreets,

Cordela Norwood or if your budget is flexible and contemporary is your taste, consider Artotel or the flasher Kosenda Hotel.

Where is Dreamtel
Dreamtel

17–19 Jalan Johar, Menteng, Jakarta

T: (0213) 928 728 F: (0213) 161 713

enquiry@dreamteljakarta.com

Coordinates (for GPS): 106º49'50.94" E, 6º11'14.84" S

Room rates: 400,000 to 1,000,000 Rp

Kota Tua

The appeal of staying in the "old city" is being relatively close to some of Jakarta's historic sites and also for the back lane quirky vibe. The downside is getting to anything else will involve dealing with the city's traffic.

The Packer Lodge

Rooms and the pod-style dorms are extremely clean and well looked after, while the hostel is loaded with open and social areas where travellers can meet one another or chat away to the friendly owner, whom you'll most likely run into in the top floor cafe.

Originally a family home, the building was first converted into warehousing and then later into the hostel you'll see they've kept the freight lift out back, which is now used to store backpacks. There's good attention to detail here a hand-drawn map explains sights to see nearby and plenty of information pertaining to greater Indonesia is mounted on the walls.

We went for a private room with bathroom over one of the dorms and were happy with both the space and the cleanliness of it. Furnished in Ikea style, there is plenty of space for your pack, a small flatscreen TV and a clean hot-water bathroom area. Our room was windowless. If you've stayed in a pod-style hostel before, you'll be well familiar with the pods here. They're solid and quite spacious with privacy curtains and small fan units the latter is important as pods with curtains can get pretty warm, even with air-con. Shared bathrooms are immaculate.

The real asset at Packer Lodge though is the common areas. There is a mini-theatre and internet area on one floor (the hostel has hi-speed WiFi throughout) and a cafe area on the top floor. There's also a streetside area for those who'd like a couple of cold drinks but would prefer to sit outside. Luggage storage is available and staff are well informed about activities in Jakarta and can make travel arrangements as required. The one oddity is that the drinks fridge where beer and so on is sold is on the ground floor but the social area where most are drinking the beer is on the top floor.

While a simple backpacker breakfast is available on site, excellent eating beckons very nearby. Step out of the hostel, turn right and walk for 30 metres and you'll reach a good spot, Warteg Gang Mangga, while another 50 metres (take the right alley) takes you to an outstanding noodle joint, Bakmi Gang Mangga, which has an English menu delicious!

Rates for the standard a very reasonable, with a slight discount available if you book through The Packer Lodge's website direct.

While we stayed here on a previous visit in 2016, on our most recent visit to Jakarta in 2018, staff would not allow us to look inside the hostel without a confirmed booking. So please note the above is based on a prior visit, not our most recent research trip in Jakarta.

Where is The Packer Lodge
The Packer Lodge

Jl Kemurnian IV 20-22

T: (021) 629 0162

Coordinates (for GPS): 106º48'53.89" E, 6º8'45.58" S

Room rates: Under 150,000 Rp

Wonderloft Hostel

This fun and friendly hostel boasts terrific social spaces on the ground floor along with a handy mini-market attached to the building and a mix of dorms, private rooms and chill-out zones on the upper two floors. Wonderloft's relaxed and welcoming vibe is the perfect introduction to Jakarta if you are feeling a little apprehensive arriving in the mega-metropolis. The communal areas are conducive to making new friends and even the list of rules states: "be polite and say hello to everyone in the room".

High ceilings and large windows offer a sense of space and openness and the cool cement floors and colourful decor keep it clean and bright. On the ground level you can play pool, table football, hang-out in the lounges and watch a movie, use the computers or whip up a storm in the kitchen and the hostel's fridge stocks the one item the mini-market does not beer, but at mini-market prices. Tons of local info is pinned to notice boards, including walking routes and transport timetables and eager staff are ready to help with any questions. Upstairs the communal space is more chilled with blue and yellow beanbags plonked on the cool polish cement floors, a pleasant spot for a quiet read or a bit of a snooze.

Dorms and private rooms are air-con cooled and ensuite and shared facilities offer hot showers with a variety of sleeping options on offer from 8-bed mixed or female only pod-style dorms or 4-bed mixed traditional bunk style dorms to large and small private twins with ensuite or shared facilities. Pods and bunks provide personal reading lights, power points and lockers and while pods offer privacy, the bunk rooms are a little more spacious and would be excellent for a group of friends.

Twins range from windowless small bunk rooms with a share bathroom or compact with an ensuite to spacious and bright with views over the street, and all look and smell both clean and fresh. Bathrooms are basic and although a little grimy at the edges that's more to do with the age of the building than maintenance as they are regularly given the once over.

A simple breakfast is included, and you can add extras for a small cost. Towels and power adapters can be rented and sundries such as SIM cards and transport cards are available to purchase. Note that a 200,000 rupiah key deposit is required on check-in.

We think Wonderloft Hostel is terrific, the prime location and friendly atmosphere are ace in our books but if Wonderloft is fully booked, you may consider The Packer Lodge or Teduh Hostel which are both nearby, however we were unable to check them out. These hostels are well reviewed on booking sites, but have a short-sighted policy of not allowing potential walk in guests from having a quick look inside. If you'd prefer a hostel in the city centre, Konko Hostel is another excellent choice.

Where is Wonderloft Hostel
Wonderloft Hostel

6–8 Jalan Bank, Kota, Jakarta

T: (0212) 607 2218

info@wonderloft.id

Coordinates (for GPS): 106º48'45.47" E, 6º8'11.88" S

Room rates: Under 150,000 Rp

The End

www.ingramcontent.com/pod-product-compliance
Lightning Source LLC
Chambersburg PA
CBHW031105080526
44587CB00011B/839